# Moving Out On Your Own

# Moving Out On Your Own

*Reflections on Leaving Home
for the First Time*

STEVE SWANSON

Augsburg
MINNEAPOLIS

MOVING OUT ON YOUR OWN
Reflections on Leaving Home for the First Time

Scripture quotations unless otherwise noted are from the New Revised Standard Version Bible, copyright © 1989 by the Division of Christian Education of the National Council of the Churches of Christ in the USA and used by permission.

Scripture quotations noted KJV are from the King James Version.

Cover design by Cindy Cobb Olson

Library of Congress Cataloging-in-Publication Data

Swanson, Steve, 1932–
   Moving out on your own : reflections on leaving home for the first time / Steve Swanson
      p.    cm.
   Includes bibliographical references.
   ISBN 0-8066-2731-X (alk. paper)
   1. Young adults—Prayer-books and devotions—English. 2. Devotional calendars. 3. Christian life. I. Title.
BV4811.S93   1995
242'.63—dc20
                                                                        95-8357
                                                                        CIP

The paper used in this publication meets the minimum requirements of American National Standard for Information Sciences—Permanence of Paper for Printed Library Materials, ANSI Z329.48-1984.                                             ∞

Manufactured in the U.S.A.                                              AF9-2731

99    98    97    96    95        2    3    4    5    6    7    8    9    10

# A Word from the Author

If you are a teenager or young adult leaving home for the first time, *MOVING OUT ON YOUR OWN* is especially for you. You recently have been—or are about to be—launched into a larger world, into spaces more vast, more interesting, more risky, and more challenging than you have ever before experienced. Not even the sky's the limit.

When the National Aeronautics and Space Administration (NASA) gets ready for a space launch, its scientists and computer experts figure out the ideal time to begin lift-off. This ideal time, or "launch window," is designed to make sure the vehicle can get into orbit, do its job and, most importantly, return home safely.

Some of you leave home in a planned and controlled way. You spend hours with parents and counselors choosing the right college, military or civilian training program, career or job opportunity. You make arrangements with family and friends, current employer, boyfriend or girlfriend, so as to leave with as little disruption and anguish as possible. And, because you are making a careful launch, you know you always will be welcomed back.

Others of you launch forth with little or no preparation. Some of you just leave. Others break away with a gigantic family fight. You may feel less secure about your new surroundings, less sure about a welcome when you return to your old home.

Regardless of whether your launch was carefully planned, these reflections will be helpful in charting your new course. They are designed to keep you examining your pathway, to warn you of possible obstacles and temptations, and to direct you to sources of guidance, help, and comfort along the way. Even if your life seems chaotic right now, even if you seem to be making some pretty important decisions without any direction—*you are not alone.*

A NASA launch window is designed to get astronauts out into space and then get them back home safely. *MOVING OUT ON YOUR OWN* has a similar purpose— to get you off with a good launch, to help you survive out there, and to maintain firm connections with your several "homes": your home in the caring hands of God, your eternal and heavenly home, and the places and loved ones you left behind.

You have yet another home. It is not behind you, but out there in the future. Whether you know it or not, this future home is one of the main reasons you are leaving behind the places of your childhood. You will make that future home together with the person or the people you love. The decisions you make now, the life you live now, will help to shape the kind of home you build in your future.

You need *all* these homes. Trust me on that.

Steve Swanson
Northfield, Minnesota

# "Fell Down, Got Up"

The Lord said to Joshua, "Stand up! Why have you fallen upon your face?"

JOSHUA 7:10

Selmer Swanson of Minneapolis (we are not related) coached ski jumpers for 40 years. Among his protégés were a dozen national champions and several Olympic jumpers. When asked how he himself learned to ski, Swanson answered: "Fell down, got up, fell down, got up."

One woman skier reminisced, "Jumping taught us to be confident of our own bodies and of ourselves, and of our ability to do something quite difficult."

Leaving for college, military service, or your first full-time job can also be difficult. You have a lot to learn, and you want to do well. Living away from your family and friends, your community and other support systems, means you will be taking new risks. And that means a lot of falling down. Your near future will be full of missed opportunities, of misunderstandings, of misguided choices, and of mischosen friends. Failure will haunt you.

In life we all fall continually. You probably have already. You got up. You will fall again. You will get up again. You must get up.

The Gospel of Jesus reminds us that we can have help getting up. God's loving hand reaches for us each time we fall, a hand that lifts us up, forgives us, brushes off the dirt, and helps us on our way again.

---

*Lord Jesus, teach me to reach out for your hand. Keep me starting again—as often as I must.*

---

# Shaped Stone

"You are Peter, and on this rock I will build my church."

MATTHEW 16:18

I watched as the earthmovers rebuilding our street lifted out a stone the size of a Volkswagen bug. That stone had a "wow" quality about it, monolithic, earthy, natural.

A sculptor can often see a more refined and shapely beauty inside such a stone. His or her work is to chip away the surrounding stone to release that inner form. "The more the marble wastes away," Michelangelo once said, "the more the statue grows."

You are not a block of marble, but rather a sculpture in progress; you are partly shaped, but not yet fully formed into what you will become. Perhaps you or those who love you pray for more of your inner talent and energy and beauty to be released.

The next few years will be a perfect time for that to happen. You are at last on your own, free to try your wings, to study, to practice, to work at and develop some of the talents and abilities that may have been dormant at home. You will have failures, of course, and false starts. God will help, though, sculpting you into a creature more useful and more beautiful.

God has sketches for each of us and can fashion us more and more into creatures who match that design. Be patient. Try not to resist your own shaping. Let the chips fall where they may.

---

*Dear God, shape me daily toward more inward beauty and more outward usefulness.*

# Carried on the Hip

Likewise the Spirit helps us in our weakness; for we do not know how to pray as we ought, but that very Spirit intercedes with sighs too deep for words.

ROMANS 8:26

Often we feel so alone. We look around us and see no one who understands, no one who seems willing or able to listen, no one who seems to care whether we even *exist*.

When we are feeling this way, the words of Romans 8:26 can help. We are reminded of a friend, an advocate, someone like a brother or sister who represents us before God, and who carries us before God.

One of the images I like to bring up when I'm thinking of the Holy Spirit carrying me is from West African tribal culture. We Westerners have many things to learn about family life from other cultures. Anthropologist Laura Bohannan describes West African babies who are handed over to an older brother or sister or cousin when they are about six months old. Pleased and proud of being given this responsibility, the guardians gently nurture the baby, never speaking an angry word or using any harsh discipline.

Bohannan said she occasionally would see an old man point to another even *older* man and say, "He is the brother who carried me on his hip." The tie is more sacred than blood.

If we could, in our dark moods, conjure up that image of the Holy Spirit carrying us on the hip, loneliness would lose a lot of its terror, and we would be back to feeling good about who we are.

---

*Holy Spirit, remind me that you are there, especially when I am feeling alone and nearing despair. Carry me on your hip. Pray for me with sighs too deep for words.*

---

# I Want

"Whoever wishes to be great among you must be your servant, and whoever wishes to be first among you must be your slave."

MATTHEW 20:26-27

Those soon to graduate from colleges, universities, or technical schools often spend their springtime waiting for letters from companies, corporations, or graduate schools. Those who aren't graduating arrange to go back to last year's summer job or look for a new one. Everyone is broke and everywhere the haunting voices echo, "I want, I want."

For students who have spent precious years and hard-earned money preparing for a career and for the good life—and who are deeply in debt—the "I want" attitude is not unusual.

Every afternoon, Saul Bellow's middle-aged, upper-class hero in *Henderson the Rain King* heard a voice whispering, "I want, I want, I want." He made peace with his "I want" in Africa, in a new culture, even sharing a cage with a tiger.

You also will have tigers to face—probably not caged and probably not in Africa. Henderson reached middle age before he faced his tiger. Then he went home and changed his life. You could start earlier. Like Mother Theresa, who considers herself only a small pencil in the hands of God, you too can turn lifetime "I want" decisions into invitations to service: "Someone needs."

Consider taking your first job with a volunteer, missionary, or service organization. The work can be very satisfying and often leads to related opportunities, sometimes to a lifetime career. There is a little bit of Mother Theresa's pencil in all of us.

---

*Transform, Lord, some of my "I wants" into "I want . . . to serve."*

# All God's Children

"Lord, when was it that we saw you hungry and gave you food, or thirsty and gave you something to drink?" ... "Truly I tell you, just as you did it to one of the least of these who are members of my family, you did it to me."

MATTHEW 25: 37, 40

Maya Angelou is an amazing woman. Her autobiography, *I Know Why the Caged Bird Sings,* tells of a troubled and mottled youth, and only partly explains the wise and deep and spiritual woman she has become in middle age. Angelou once wrote:

I am freed by knowing I'm a child of God. I am burdened by knowing that everyone else is also.

You will be bombarded in the next years by religious groups and denominations who want your allegiance and your money. Beware of those groups that teach you to focus only on yourself, that give you only the inward and the upward look.

The essence of Jesus' message is the outward look. That's what Maya Angelou meant by her "burden." She feels, and we ought to feel, what Jesus *wants* us to feel—the burden of the world's needs. Everyone out there is a child of God. When we feed the hungry, clothe the naked, welcome the stranger, visit the prisoner, or do any other act of mercy, even to those who may seem the least worthy—*especially* to those who seem the least worthy—we are doing it, Jesus says, to the King, the Lord, to God himself.

A life of service is not Christ's command; it is his invitation.

---

*S*how me, Lord, the needs of the least of your children, and how I can help meet those needs.

---

# The Book of Life

Now Jesus did many other signs ... which are not written in this book. But these are written that you may come to believe ... and that through believing may have life in his name.

JOHN 20:30-31

The heroine in Olive Schreiner's novel, *The Story of an African Farm* (1900), in her hunger for learning says, "Books. They shall tell me all, all, all."

Lifetime learning that begins now can make you more understanding, more whole, and more useful to your natural world, to its people, and to God your creator.

Follow your instinct to learn. Let curiosity lead you. Interested in animals, birds, railroads, your own mind? There are books. Curious about God? There is a book. It is written to help us believe—and have life.

Our curiosity about God and the Bible should nudge us toward daily Bible study. To avoid faltering or false starts, we need a good plan.

A plan starts with picking a time of day—maybe first thing in the morning or last thing at night. Then choose an approach. There are books on how to read the Bible. You could also ask a Bible teacher or pastor or Christian friend how and where to start. One of the quickest ways to get started is just to ask a half dozen Christian friends, "What are your four or five favorite books in the Bible?"

Pick the favorites most often mentioned, be faithful about your daily study time, and you're on your blessed way.

---

*Dear Lord, make me a lifetime learner—and especially one who studies and meditates upon your Word.*

---

# Princes and Sheep Shearers

I say to everyone among you not to think of yourself more highly
than you ought to think.

ROMANS 12:3

Sybylla, the feisty heroine of Miles Franklin's
autobiographical novel, *My Brilliant Career* (1901), struggled not
only with the strictures of turn-of-the-century Australian
womanhood, but with her attitudes toward the several social
levels she frequented. "To venerate a person simply for his
position," she says, "I never did or will. To me the Prince of
Wales is no more important than a sheep shearer."

Some people give themselves permission to feel and act
superior, to be proud and smug and self-satisfied. The word
*sophomoric* (look it up) was coined on a college campus when
some partially-educated person began putting on airs.

Winning the conference championship, investing four years in
a college education or four more in an advanced degree, or
being a soloist in the choir or first chair in the orchestra does not
earn you or anyone else a snob license. Think back to the
teachers, mentors, and coaches who seemed to you the most
educated and capable. Weren't they also the most humble—the
most willing to listen and to take your ideas seriously?

Christ, who was all wisdom and all power and all goodness,
set an example of humility by emptying himself and walking the
way of the cross (Philippians 2:5-11).

Treat princes and sheep shearers alike, no matter how many
honors you earn. You could learn a lot from a sheep shearer.

---

*Teach me, patient Lord, to treat everyone I meet not only equally,
but pleasantly.*

---

# No John Waynes

"The Lord does not see as mortals see; they look on the outward appearance, but the Lord looks on the heart."

The men I have known have never been John Wayne," the writer Joan Didion once wrote. Wayne and other larger-than-life sports, Hollywood, and TV heroes and heroines create faulty expectations and lead to faulty decisions, such as what those we might love should look and act like, what we and others should wear, how much we should weigh, what constitutes an adventure or a romance, and how long it should take to solve a problem.

Even if we have lived our youthful years in a capsule—a small town, a small college, a strict family—our lives are more real than film or TV life. John Wayne's movies are a dream world, not our world.

Our problems will not surge to either satisfying or tragic conclusions in a predictable TV half hour or a film's ninety minutes. The same problems will nag at most of us for an entire lifetime.

Those we befriend and love, and who care about us, will be as ordinary and faultridden as we ourselves are. Joan Didion learned, as we must learn, that no John Waynes will "take us to the bend in the river where the cottonwoods grow."

Even more than our truest friends, Christ sees us as we really are and offers his forgiving love to each of us—problems and all.

---

*Teach me, dear Lord, as I am bombarded by impossible models, to try harder to appreciate who my friends and I really are.*

# *Your Natural Place*

"The earth is the Lord's and all that is in it, the world, and those who live in it."

PSALM 24:1

Back in about 1915, writer Isak Dinesen (Baronness Karen Blixen) with great difficulty transported twelve fine peony bulbs from her home in Denmark and planted them on her farm in Africa. The first—and only—white flower that bloomed, she immediately cut and proudly displayed in a vase.

Only later did she learn from her gardener friend, Lady McMillan, that peonies had never before bloomed or produced seed in Africa. Her solitary flower could have been the first of a whole strain of native peonies. Dinesen could have had a flower named after her and been the mother of new and perennial beauty in Africa.

Beauty has a way of looking best where it blooms naturally. Dinesen's mistake is often our own mistake—trying to pluck beauty from nature, putting it in an unnatural setting for our own pleasure. Did you ever, when you were little, bring in and try to feed a baby bird or rabbit, only to watch it die?

You and I are just as unique as Dinesen's white peony. We, too, can bloom where we are planted if we are satisfied to let the Spirit help us grow into who we were intended to be.

All of God's creation has its own place and its own beauty and serves a necessary function in the wholeness of God's plan. Through prayer and attentiveness to God's answers, we can usually discover our natural place.

---

*Teach me, Lord, to cherish the fullness of your world, to appreciate natural beauty, and to bloom where I am planted.*

---

# Just a Game

The treacherous are taken captive by their schemes.

PROVERBS 11:6

Minnesota Twins Manager Tom Kelley sent winning pitcher Jack Morris back into the tenth inning of a scoreless World Series game, saying, "What the heck. It's just a game."

There are useful lessons in games: setting goals, being a good sport, playing by the rules, being a team player. Indeed, St. Paul compares the struggle and the training of an athlete to the Christian life (1 Corinthians 9:24-27).

But sports can also have some unsavory side effects: winning at all costs, beating—even humiliating—an opponent, fudging on the rules.

We use sports words every day: we want to "make a hit." We set "goals." We cry "foul." We "make a pitch." We say "she's a knockout." A young man back in his apartment or dorm room after a date might be asked, "Did you score?"

Although both men and women sometimes want romance to be "the game of love," our sexual decisions are far too important to be seen only as a game.

If making love *were* a game, then maybe it should be more like baseball, where no score going into extra innings may be the best game we have ever enjoyed; or like golf, where the lowest score is the best and where "1" is considered perfect. Perhaps love's coveted ring goes to those whose lifetime score is low, maybe 1 or, for the time being, even 0.

---

*Teach me Lord, to examine my attitudes toward games and life, especially my sex life.*

---

# *Balancing Act*

"Cursed is the ground because of you."

Evelyn Minshull captures in her novel *Eve* the human spirit caught between a desire to be perfect and having to struggle through sinfulness, weakness, and failure toward life's only *partial* successes. In her story, both Adam and Eve long to return to Eden, but find life on the outside more challenging than Eden's "eternal childlikeness."

Life apart from God is more than challenging. It is impossible. The biblical story of Eden reminds us that from the beginning of human experience, any hope we have of goodness, achievement, or satisfaction will always be dashed by sin. Knowing and accepting God's forgiveness and love is the only way we can keep that harsh truth from driving us deeply and eternally into despair.

Walking daily in the forgiveness won by Christ on the cross gives us hope. The stains of Eden, the corruption of a fallen human nature, are washed from us by Word and sacrament. By our sinful selves we can do nothing. With Christ by our side, we can say with St. Paul, "I can do all things in him who strengthens me" (Philippians 4:13).

Life thus becomes a balancing act between the beckoning of our sinful natures and the evil one, and the awareness that Christ is in us, stengthening us daily, hourly, moment by moment.

---

*Teach me, gentle Savior, to recognize your power inside me and to call upon you in every temptation and need.*

---

# *Learning to Listen*

Eli said to Samuel, "Go, lie down; and if he calls you, you shall say, 'Speak, Lord, for your servant is listening.'"

I SAMUEL 3:9

A good conversationalist—someone we find easy to talk to—is most likely a good listener: one who asks leading questions, draws us out, and then listens carefully to our answers or responses. We enjoy such people because they seem truly interested in us.

Listening is a prime characteristic of the Christian: listening to God, to the collective voice of the church, to our best inner voice, and to each other.

We are reminded by the story of the boy Samuel that when God calls we need to listen. We learn that if we are going to pray, we certainly ought to listen for answers.

It's pretty easy when we're young to shrug off the organized church, to find our spiritual life alone or with a small group of friends. But the church often has a collective and historical voice worth listening to. My problems and concerns of today were probably someone else's years ago. How were they handled and solved back then? Can I learn from that?

Each of us has something called a conscience. Although a conscience can be misguided and perverted, at its best our inner voice is a medium of the Holy Spirit that can warn and guide us. We need to listen to it.

Finally, we Christians must learn to listen to each other. How can we help, befriend, or share the Gospel sensibly if we don't listen to one another?

---

*L*ord, *make me a listener. Teach me to learn from listening.*

---

# One Special Place

After Jesus had spoken these words, he went out with his disciples across the Kidron valley, to a place where there was a garden, which he and his disciples entered.

JOHN 18:1-2

The Garden of Gethsemane is still a beautiful spot, Bethany on one side and old Jerusalem on the other. Jesus went there so often that Judas picked that very place to betray him.

Gardens are often places of retreat, of contemplation, of communion with nature and with God. The gardens of England, Japan, and the castles of France are world-renowned.

Each of us has a garden, a retreat. Perhaps as you leave home you are leaving your special place behind: your backyard, a vine-covered front porch, the neighbor's orchard.

Find another. Jesus needed a quiet place of retreat; so do we. We need from time to time to get away, to commune with God, to pray, and to listen for messages from the Spirit. The busier our lives become—and what time in life is busier than when you first leave home, struggling to make your way, with no parent or anyone else to help—the more we need a quiet place.

Your garden need not be abundant with nature. A chapel will do, a park bench, or maybe even a few plants clustered in a corner of your room or apartment.

Of course we should be able to commune with God anywhere and at any time; but if Jesus found one special place worth going back to again and again, maybe our devotional life could benefit from that, too.

---

*Lord Jesus, as you found solace in the quiet of a garden, show me my garden, my special place, where I can become closer to you and to your Word.*

---

# Responsible Sexuality

"Everyone who looks at a woman with lust has already committed adultery with her in his heart."

MATTHEW 5:28

In an essay called "Brothers and Sisters," writer Alice Walker tells how she was forbidden to watch their farm animals mate, a pastime that filled her brothers with "an aimless sort of lust" and urged them into town on Saturday nights encouraged by their father. As they grew older, her brothers became more and more sexually irresponsible—all but one brother, Jason.

> Jason is the only one of my brothers [she wrote] who assumes responsibility for all his children. The other four all fathered children . . . nieces and nephews whom I will probably never know.

Only Alice Walker and her oldest brother, Jason, shed no tears at her father's funeral. He had set his sons a bad example and encouraged them in bad directions, and they knew it.

Youthful irresponsibility of any kind—but particularly sexual irresponsibility—often has profound and lasting consequences. These years away from home may seem to offer freedom from rules and restrictions, but there is no freedom from the consequences of our actions. Patterns of promiscuity may be hard to break later; and their all-too-frequent consequences— shallow relationships, pregnancy, abortion, and sexually transmitted diseases—can not only mess up yours and others' present lives, but also your futures.

---

*Lord Jesus, make me a responsible person in every way, especially sexually.*

---

# *Forgiving and Honoring*

Honor your father and your mother.

EXODUS 20:12

When I see a mother hitting a kid in a supermarket," writes attorney Paul Mones of Santa Monica, California, "I say something."

Mones' work has made him especially sensitive to child abuse. For over twenty years he has been defending juveniles in criminal cases. Today he is the only lawyer in the country who specializes in defending juveniles accused of killing their fathers or mothers.

Mones's clients typically are teenagers who, having been abused since childhood and pushed to the abyss by fear and anger, lash out in self defense—and kill.

The privileges and responsibilities of parenthood are extensive and profound, as many of you have learned from your own parents and will someday perhaps learn for yourselves. All parents make mistakes; but those who abandon, belittle, batter, or sexually abuse their children scarcely deserve to be subjects of the law Moses brought down from the mountaintop: "Honor your father and your mother" (Exodus 20:12).

If you have been hurt or abused by your parents, the answer is not to hurt back, but to try to understand and forgive—and to ask for God's help in seeking care and healing.

If you have been raised with love and concern by one or both parents, you have reason to thank God most profoundly.

---

*Teach me, Lord, to look at my parents honestly—thanking, accepting, and forgiving as you give me the strength and understanding to do so.*

---

# Heroines and Heroes

Show yourself in all respects a model of good works.

TITUS 2:7

In her popular book, *Can Molly Ivins Say That?*, outspoken and outrageous Dallas journalist Ivins takes on the "sumbitches" [sic] in national politics as easily as she deals with the ludicrous cries of "exploitation" by the Dallas Cowgirls or the macho chauvinism of local "bubbas."

Ivins expresses, in a particularly moving chapter, her profound admiration for the varied but superb competence of six women who are mayors of major Texas cities, each one a heroine, each worth emulating.

As women are rethinking their traditional roles, heroines for young women are as scarce as heroes are for men. Young men have watched as male athletes' stars have flamed out in bouts of King Kong sex and commercial sellout; as more and more male politicians are exposed as corrupt and unprincipled harassers; and as professors, clergy, and scientists topple.

Young women and young men do need heroes and heroines; but they soon learn that every human being has flaws and weaknesses. The only true goodness is from God. Only in Jesus can we find a true model of the ideas and principles around which to fashion our lives.

*Teach me, Lord, to build my own image after your example.*

# *Peacemaking Possibilities*

"Blessed are the peacemakers."

MATTHEW 5:9

President Jimmy Carter called the United States "the only superpower left on earth." Wherever he speaks, he reminds us of that awesome responsibility and exhorts us to be peacemakers.

One of our least popular in-office presidents, Jimmy Carter has become our most popular out-of-office president—the living president, one pollster discovered, with whom most Americans would enjoy having lunch.

Can we credit his popularity to the Carter Center's promotion of peace, democracy, human rights, earth care, and disease prevention? Or to his wielding a hammer for Habitat for Humanity? Perhaps he just seems like a good person, someone we might *enjoy* lunching with.

If their deeds are large enough, both the famous and the infamous are remembered in history books—both those who start wars or who, like Carter, work for peace. Hitler, Napoleon, and Hannibal are remembered, but so are Mother Theresa, Dr. King, and Gandhi.

Your name may not go into a history book, but you can make a lifetime impression by exercising love and care and peacemaking in even the smallest of ways. The "little" people we tend to remember are those who, in our town, on our block, in our school, or in our workplace, have quietly gone about making life better.

How do you want to be forgotten or remembered?

---

*Show me, Holy Spirit, how to uncover the peacemaking possibilities in myself.*

---

# When Language Fails

"You have heard that it was said, 'You shall love your neighbor and hate your enemy.' But I say to you, love your enemies and pray for those who persecute you."

MATTHEW 5:43-44

How could Elie Wiesel, who suffered so much at the hands of the Nazis, come out of Auschwitz proclaiming that "even hate of hatred is dangerous"?

"Hatred," Wiesel says, "is not only destructive, it is *self*-destructive."

Most people will never be subjected to the cruelty that Wiesel had to endure, but we should listen when he admonishes us to learn to communicate. "We resort to violence," he says, "when language fails." When we can't talk our way beyond violence—or worse, when we use words to ignore, condone, or even encourage the evil within and around us—then hatred and other base emotions will surface and take over our lives, plunging us into anguish just as surely as did a concentration camp for Wiesel.

Language is not only a vehicle of prayer for speaking to and listening to God. Language is also the bridge to human understanding ("What exactly did you mean by that?"), encouragement ("Good for you!"), and good relationships ("I'm sorry; let's talk about that").

Only through language can we seek the positive in ourselves, learning through God's Word and through prayer to love our enemies, to practice forgiveness and self control, to build relationships, and to seek inner peace.

---

*Empower me, O God, to quell my basest inner emotions, replacing them with the language of forgiveness, peace, and self-control.*

---

# No Enthusiasm

Saul was ravaging the church by entering house after house; dragging off both men and women, he committed them to prison.

ACTS 8:3

Saul was an enthusiastic persecuter of the church until the voice of Jesus confronted him on the Damascus road and his enthusiasm was redirected to more positive goals.

Award-winning architect Ed Sovik has also directed his life enthusiastically toward positive goals. It started when he was fifteen. Fellow students at their mission school in China invited him to join them at midnight in throwing eggs into the open window of their sleeping headmaster's quarters. "I liked the headmaster," Sovik said, "and had no enthusiasm for the act—though I did it."

Soon afterward, however, he was so ashamed that, as he said, "I decided that for the rest of my life I would never do anything that I could not do with enthusiasm."

Peer pressure can get us into all kinds of unsavory, embarrassing, and even illegal acts. When a group gets together, its mind is usually a notch or two lower on the moral and ethical scale than any one of its members alone. That's why college and university fraternities—and occasionally sororities—the Ku Klux Klan, and military and fraternal conventions sometimes make headlines. We may, when in a group, do things for which we would have very little enthusiasm when alone.

Living the Christ-like life means examining our every act, no matter how many "friends" we do it with.

---

*Help me always, Lord, to measure my acts against my God-given enthusiasm for doing them.*

---

# *Trust Me*

Whoever walks with the wise becomes wise, but the companion of fools suffers harm.

PROVERBS 13:20

Millions of people liked Hitler—at first. He was not, they learned later, what he seemed.

New friends sometimes seem pretty OK too—at first. "Trust me," they say. And we do—at first.

Back in our hometown schools and neighborhoods, at least we could get to know friends slowly.

You have learned, or will soon learn, that colleges and schools, new towns and new jobs, are havens of instant friendships. You are assigned roommates and co-learners and co-workers. You meet new people in lectures, on teams, in work crews, and on lunch breaks. Without enough time to test new friends, you are apt, nevertheless, to "grapple them to your soul," as Polonius says in *Hamlet,* "with hoops of steel."

Away from home, and separated from *old* friends, we so desperately want *new* ones. Take all that wanting, add the instant trust of new surroundings, and throw in the rampant desire to "have fun," and you will know why campuses and other workplaces of the young and unmarried often are riddled with immorality, promiscuity, and date rape.

"Trust me."

We are designed for friendship with God and with others, but God also gave us wisdom, and caution, and insight.

---

*Help me, Guardian Lord, to examine my need for friendship and to be careful about the new friends I am making.*

---

# The Gift of Language

From the same mouth come blessing and cursing . . . this ought not
to be so.

JAMES 3:10

Prospero, the hero in Shakespeare's *The Tempest,* taught the
bestial Caliban to speak. After their falling out, Caliban said to
his mentor: "You taught me language, and my profit on it is, I
know how to curse." Thereafter Caliban cursed Prospero
constantly:

> All the infections that the sun sucks up
> From bogs, fens, flats, on Prospero fall and make him
> Inch by inch a disease.

Language and communication are such powerful gifts that we
attribute them to creatures we deem most intelligent: whales,
dolphins, wolves, bees. Language, our most human of abilities,
can raise our sights higher or, like Caliban, make us more
bestial. We judge people by their language, and they judge us by
ours. Language can edify and exalt; it can also debase and
offend. With words we understand, and with words we decide.
We can speak words of blessing and praise or blasphemy and
cursing. The name of God and words of unspeakable vulgarity
can pass over the same lips.

Language is also the stuff of human relationships: "I'm sorry."
"Nice job." "Can I help?" "You look terrific." "Tell me about it."
Such phrases solidify friendships and often lead us onto paths of
service and help.

---

*Thank you, Lord, for the gift of language. Remind me daily to
examine my language and chasten it.*

---

# *Final Exam*

Blessed is anyone who endures temptation. Such a one has stood the test and will receive the crown of life that the Lord has promised to those who love him.

JAMES 1:12

You have been in school and know about final exams. They can be terrifying. Decades from now, you may still have recurring nightmares about walking stone-cold unprepared into an exam.

Teachers who try to reduce terror by teaching without exams or grades soon confront endless procrastination.

Much of what we really need in life, the knowledge most vitally important, will never appear on any exam. The final you take in a human sexuality course will not necessarily prepare you for what to do and say in the backseat of a car or alone in an apartment when the hormones are running hot. Neither will the hours you spend practicing for a driver's test teach you how to react when you're skidding sideways toward an oncoming semi or what to say when a close friend, eighty-five percent drunk, wants to drive you home. Only schooling in God's word and in prayer can help us pass these real-life exams—and maybe asking that our angels continually watch over us.

Life tests us in so many ways. What your grandma might have called "trials and tribulations"—the ups and downs of friendship, love, work, marriage, parenting, illness, and even death—gradually shape us into who we are and what we will be.

Might not the lesser exams of life be helping prepare us for a last judgment, our ultimate final exam?

---

*Show me, caring Lord, not only what I am expected to learn but also what I need and ought to learn.*

---

# Reaching Out

Put away from you all bitterness and wrath and anger and wrangling and slander.

EPHESIANS 4:31

George Eliot's classic novel *Silas Marner* (1861) portrays a weaver falsely accused of theft. Year after year he became more bitter, reclusive, and miserly. Marner lived alone, shunned society, and hoarded gold. One night his gold was stolen. He had little time to lament his loss, however, for a homeless, golden-haired little girl appeared at his door.

Marner took this replacement gold into his cottage and raised her as his own daughter. Slowly his thoughts and life turned outward as his love for little Eppie grew.

All of us can remember the enduring hurt of bitter scenes in which we were misjudged, lied about, abused, or victimized. Perhaps we too started hoarding gold: reclusiveness, overwork, academic or athletic or artistic achievements, prizes, and awards.

Anger, selfishness, bitterness, and reclusiveness can turn us more and more inside ourselves, set us on selfish pursuits, and shut out neighborliness, friendship, and love.

A golden child may not appear at your door, but there is other gold: Big Brother/Big Sister challenges, volunteer work, friends who need help. Golden opportunities. As we reach out to others with love and understanding and help, our misery-turned-inward can be cured—because, of course, helping others is God's work.

---

*Dear Lord, show me, even in the midst of my busy activity, those people that I could care about and help.*

---

# Promise of Freedom

If the Son makes you free, you will be free indeed.

JOHN 8:36

There are so many ways to be free: drug free, debt free, toll free, worry free, pain free. Freedom is a precious heritage that, by definition, comes with our citizenship: "We are endowed by our Creator with certain inalienable rights...life, liberty, and the pursuit of happiness."

Because of Abraham Lincoln (who said "I wish that all persons, everywhere, could be free"), the Emancipation Proclamation, the bloody Civil War, and the Thirteenth Amendment, people are no longer sent out to work as slaves at the point of a gun or the tip of a whip. Our inalienable right to liberty means that no one ought to be able to tell anyone else where to live or where to work—or when or for whom.

But other slaveries have arisen: drug and chemical abuse, discrimination, intimidation, coercion, harassment, job security, and most common of all, the slaveries of both poverty and wealth.

Your training and education contain freedom's promise. As you leave home and move out into the larger world, you can be empowered to resist all forms of slavery that would entrap you and others. Your Creator has endowed you with that right. Don't step from freedom into other forms of slavery: alcohol, drugs, sex, work, study. Anything done at the wrong time or in excess can lead to slavery.

---

*Teach me, Lord, to cherish my freedoms and the freedoms of all others. Make me thankful for those who have lived and died to make them possible.*

---

# What's in a Name?

A disciple is not above the teacher, but everyone who is fully qualified will be like the teacher.

LUKE 6:40

Iris (Siri spelled backwards), the heroine in Siri Hustvedt's 1992 novel *The Blindfold*, has an affair with her professor but, because he started out as her teacher, she scarcely dares to call him by his first name:

> It was not easy calling Professor Rose Michael. . . . Universities may be the last places in America where first names still have the force of intimacy.

Teacher and student, boss and employee, clergy and parishioner often discuss, exchange ideas, and work cooperatively many hours a week, sometimes for years. Working so closely is both a privilege and a responsibility.

The adults with whom you work will resonate with your energy and eager young talent. You will respect and work hard for them because they take you and your ideas seriously. Maybe no one has ever done that before.

The use of titles has always been one of society's ways of sorting out relationships and protecting the powerless from the powerful. After weeks of working together on a project, it may seem superfluous, even ridiculous for you to keep calling your older co-worker Dr., Professor, Pastor, even Sir, Ma'am, Mr., Mrs., or Ms. Continuing to use titles may make sense, however, in keeping your roles straight, your relationships healthy, and the boundaries between you properly drawn.

---

*Lord, show me how to keep in balance my relationships with those with whom and for whom I work.*

---

# *Choose for Yourself*

"You must choose, and not I."

The late Margaret Laurence, a Canadian novelist, has been called the best stylist writing in English. In her novel *A Jest of God* (1966), Laurence's Rachel, an unmarried teacher, has never made choices. She has just let life "happen to her" and later regrets it. She says:

> All of my life seems a chance encounter, but everything that happens to me is permanent. That isn't a very clever way to be.

If you are very skilled or talented or personable, if you learn to be very good at what you do, you may never have to apply for a job; you may never have to decide which project to undertake; you may never have to seek out friends; you may never even be able to choose who to like or love or work for or with.

One of the serious truths of life is this: if you don't make choices for yourself, someone else will make them for you. God has a plan for your life, and it is often possible to recognize that plan as it unfolds. But others have plans for you as well. Some of them are *not* God's plan.

Having people who want to direct your work and your love and your life is heady business—but so also is making your own life choices. Because others may not recognize God's plan for you, seek it out for yourself. Stay close to God through Word, worship, and prayer. Listen carefully. Then choose for yourself. Don't let others make all your delicious choices.

---

*S*how me, gentle Spirit, how my life choices need to be made and who needs to make them.

---

# Finding the Right One

Therefore a man leaves his father and his mother and clings to his wife, and they become one flesh.

GENESIS 2:24

If you choose to marry, finding the right person at the right time will be of great importance. Getting away from home by moving out on your own offers a new menu. For starters, you leave a comfortable but perhaps not fully-satisfying hometown honey. Now you can examine marriage, study how God feels about it, and start to list the qualities you will look for in a mate—mentally creating a custom design.

What qualities will you want in your custom-designed spouse? Do you want a fashion plate with money, position, a house on the hill? Or do you want a combination of love, friendship, communication, a good parent, a sense of humor? You may not be able to have both models.

"How can I find that right person?" you ask. First of all, pray. Ask God (1) to help you recognize that person when he or she comes along, and (2) to help shape you into someone your dreamboat will want to love. Then, (3) when you date, study the person: discuss values, get beyond small talk and shallow subjects.

The second point is where you have some control. If you want clean-cut and nifty, then rethink your grunge wardrobe and hairdo. If you want spiritual, be more spiritual. If you want kind and thoughtful, be kind and thoughtful. Likes attract as often as unlikes; and pollsters tell us that, in marriage at least, the more we have in common, the better our chances.

---

*Dear Lord, lead me to the person I should marry, and make me ready for that moment.*

---

# *Urgent or Eternal?*

"You are worried and distracted by many things; there is need of only one thing."

LUKE 10:41

Busy-ness is epidemic. With days and nights so busy (even busy dreams), we have no solitude, no time to think or reflect, no time to develop our spiritual and inner selves. Stress and anxiety result, along with a nagging sense of getting farther and farther behind.

John LeCarre, best-selling writer of espionage and thriller novels, writes in his book *A Murder of Quality* (1961):

> I know a dozen people who would pay you thirty thousand a year for telling them every day that what is important is seldom urgent. Urgent equals ephemeral, and ephemeral equals unimportant.

The opposite of ephemeral is eternal. St. Paul describes love in 1 Corinthians 13 by saying: "love never ends." Why not invest our lives in St. Paul's never-ending "fruits of the spirit":

> love, joy, peace, patience, kindness, goodness, faithfulness, gentleness, self-control. There is no law against such things. GALATIANS 5:22

The ephemeral fruits? Position, power, popularity, money, fame. God couldn't care less about these. Maybe *we* should care less. Reflect on your busy activities. Rank them on a chart with ETERNAL at the top and EPHEMERAL at the bottom. Find time for prayer and meditation, for kindness, goodness, gentleness, and loving service by sloughing off the useless stuff at the bottom of your list.

---

*Wise and insightful Spirit, shape my days toward what is eternal.*

---

# Let Peace Begin

They shall beat their swords into plowshares, and their spears into pruning hooks; nation shall not lift up sword against nation, neither shall they learn war any more.

ISAIAH 2:4

Good and faithful people in every generation have hoped and prayed and worked for peace. Nevertheless, one world peace organization estimates that about 50 brush-fire wars are being fought in any given year.

War seems to start with greedy people who hope to profit from it, with power-hungry people who hope to rise to prominence because of it, or with stubborn and prejudiced people who want to force their beliefs and practices on others.

Although these are the people who *start* the wars, they usually are not the people who *fight* them.

If only middle-aged and affluent men had to fight, if mothers and grandmothers could choose, if the young were asked whether they *wanted* to die, there would be few wars.

During Operation Desert Storm, an effort to free Kuwait (and Kuwait's oil) from Iraq's domination, PFC Aaron Howard said, "War is terrible, and there are no such things as heroes."

Some will argue that the Hitlers of the world need to be stopped. A counterargument is that in a world where negotiation and world order prevails, a Hitler could never rise to power in the first place. Peace starts in the minds of each of us as we root out greed, hatred, prejudice, and religious and political intolerance.

---

*L*ord, let there be peace on earth, and let it begin with me.

---

# *Talking and Listening*

Come now, let us argue it out.

ISAIAH 1:18

How do you make a love relationship work? With togetherness? With passion? By becoming more and more physical? By doing things together: movies, plays, concerts, museums, ball games, skiing, hiking?

Hard questions. Leo Buscaglia, who writes books, lectures, and teaches seminars about love and love relationships, often cites a survey in which *happily* married people listed, in order of importance, the qualities they found most valuable in making their relationships work. On 600 of the 1,000 responses, communication was listed as number one. Sex came in a lazy eighth.

When you're young, you're apt to turn those rankings around. There's a lot of chemistry in young love. The physical part seems extremely important, and waiting is difficult. I haven't forgotten. We have our mouths so full of each other's lips that there seems little opportunity to talk.

Buscaglia and others suggest that those who relate best, communicate best. The trick is to do plenty of talking and listening, learning as much as possible about the other person, before getting too physically attached.

If the most you can ever get out of your date is heavy breathing, a sigh, a grunt, or a coo, look elsewhere. Imagine spending an entire lifetime communicating at that level.

---

*Dear Lord, send me someone I can talk to.*

---

# Social Climbing

"When you are invited by someone to a wedding banquet, do not sit down at the place of honor, in case someone more distinguished than you has been invited.... For all who exalt themselves will be humbled, and those who humble themselves will be exalted."

LUKE 14:7-11

There is a bit of social climber in each of us. We like the "in" group, those who move upward and onward, the socially active and affluent. There's probably nothing inherently wrong with that. Upper-class people need friends, too.

But the mere fact that one is wealthy or prominent or well-connected doesn't make him or her an apt choice for a friend. Ann Landers wrote recently, "My heart goes out to the young woman who spent four years learning how to behave in polite society, and the rest of her life looking for that polite society."

Affluence doesn't necessarily convey politeness or goodness or warmth or deep friendships. Wealth may even nudge such things into the background. Likewise, power. "Power corrupts," Lord Acton wrote, "and absolute power corrupts absolutely." Those who have toadied to the powerful, to industrialists, political leaders, and others who are rich and famous, are often corrupted.

Jesus taught us a good lesson. He moved freely among the wealthy and powerful, but just as freely—perhaps more freely—among the derelict and downtrodden. His position and his power derived from who he was, not from whom he knew or who was financially backing him.

---

*Gentle Spirit, teach me the futility of social climbing. Give me the spirit of Jesus, to see everyone not only as equal, but as interesting and important.*

---

# Reach Out for the Mystery

"This is my body, which is given for you."

LUKE 22:19

Many of you who read this will be somewhat ticked off at the church of your childhood. Now that you are on your own, you may be choosing not to go to church. You have your reasons.

Rebellion, perhaps. Maybe you grew up in a strict home and were forced to be religious. Now no one can force you.

Hypocrisy, perhaps. Maybe you look back to your family and other adult church members and wonder why they couldn't better practice what they professed in church.

Doubt, perhaps. You aren't sure you believe all those doctrines and teachings that seemed so easy when you were young.

You may soon be ready to try church again. As you live your life as an adult, experiencing failures and the power of sin, you may see your church family with more compassion and forgiveness. We are sinners, all of us, who have no power within ourselves to be saints. We are *declared* saints, however, because of God's grace and forgiveness.

Nor can everything about God be understood. Ten of the world's best theologians gathered in one room couldn't explain even one of the mysteries of God.

"When Jesus offered us his body," says C.S. Lewis, "he said 'Take and eat,' not take and understand."

The church needs you, if for no other reason than to hear from you how it might better serve other young people who have your needs and concerns.

So come back and help us. Reach out for the mystery.

---

*Holy Spirit, give me the gift of faith and the power to forgive others for their weaknesses, even as I am forgiven for mine.*

---

# Alone and Together

After he had dismissed the crowds, he went up on the mountain by himself to pray. When evening came, he was there alone.

MATTHEW 14:23

Jesus, like all of us, needed time for meditation and prayer, time to be alone. On a number of occasions, he spent that prayer time on mountains, away from other people. But, *he always came down from the mountain*. Some of us don't—and modern technology makes it all too easy to isolate ourselves from others. Computers teach us skills and answer our questions. We can plug into networks around the world. VCRs and microwave popcorn become our movie houses. Without ever leaving home we can work, shop, go to church, and pay bills. The car phone has created mobile offices.

Many electronic gadgets are being called interactive: a person interacting with a machine. That kind of interacting seems like aloneness—pecking at a keyboard, playing video games, pushing buttons, and pulling levers. Hundreds of people in a gambling casino and each one alone—with a machine. Virtual reality is next: you see and respond to what seems like a real person in a real scene, but isn't.

The talking-to-no-one crazies on city streets are victims of too much alone-ness. So are many suicidal teenagers. We need human interaction. God fashioned us to be social creatures. We need to talk to, look at, and touch each other. E-mail is not a conversation. Faxing a diagram is not a planning meeting.

Novelist Marie Henri Beyle (Stendahl) wrote: "One can acquire everything in solitude—except character."

---

*Lord Jesus, teach me to find, as you found, a balance between my alone time and my together-with-others time.*

---

# Homelessness

"I will get up and go to my father, and I will say to him, 'Treat me like one of your hired hands.' "

LUKE 15:18-19

Homelessness can be a mental attitude. Coming from a fancy home on a suburban hillside and having every advantage can't keep you from feeling as homeless as a street person—if you do feel that way.

The God-like father in Luke 15 welcomes his returning child with open arms. Our own parents may not. Unfortunately, when we are young and most likely to rebel, our parents may be having their own marital problems and mid-life uncertainties. Their problems and ours can get terribly tangled together. An angry, homeless feeling often follows.

I guess we all feel some anger toward home. I guess we all need to reject *some* of our roots. But any rejection of home that goes on profoundly, indefinitely, and unchecked can destroy all roots, kill your branch of the family tree, and lose you a lifetime of positive family interaction.

The next few years, when you are first away from home, can be a time of healing, reestablishing, nourishing, and cherishing roots. Living away from home can soften hurts, heal wounds, and make it easier to get reacquainted with the flawed people who love you so much: your family.

Write a letter. Pick up the phone. Start fertilizing the roots in your family.

*Dear God, teach me to cherish what is good and well worth keeping about my home and family.*

# *Body Temple*

Do you not know that your body is a temple of the Holy Spirit within you, which you have from God, and that you are not your own? For you were bought with a price; therefore glorify God in your body.

1 CORINTHIANS 6:19-20

You are moving out on your own. You will be in your own apartment, in a dorm, in a new town maybe. For the first time in 20 years you can eat exactly what you want. As you walk down the cafeteria line you can skip the fruits and the salads and, if you like, take only mashed potatoes, gravy, and dessert. If you are making your own meals, you can eat pizza and Pepsi and Twinkies from now until doomsday.

But moving out on your own does not make *you* your own, as St. Paul reminds us in 1 Corinthians (above): "You are not your own; you were bought with a price."

A better approach, now that you *have* full responsibility for your own body, would be to *take* full responsibility. If you have trusted your mom for good nutrition, think back to and follow her principles. Study nutrition. Build body and spirit together. Exercise. Eat well. Avoid the poisons: alcohol, tobacco, drugs. Think well, be well.

There is nothing more beautiful, or more sought after in our society, than a healthy, robust, and youthful body. You have one. Keep it, cherish it.

Don't take it from me; take it from God: "Your body is a temple of the Holy Spirit within you."

---

*Holy Spirit, help me to recognize my body as your temple and to keep it a fit dwelling for you.*

---

# Living Miracles

Remember your creator in the days of your youth, before the days of trouble come, and the years draw near, when you will say, "I have no pleasure in them."

ECCLESIASTES 12:1

Back when the writer of Ecclesiastes wrote these lines, youth was a time of joy and freedom. The picture he is creating is of a child growing out of youthful freedom and pleasure into the complicated and difficult days when an adult would say, "Where's all the fun gone?"

Times have changed. Growing up has become much more difficult than it once was. The lives of the young are riddled with abuse, anguish, drugs, sex, violence. Most grownups look at what the young must endure today, shake their heads and say, "I'm glad I grew up back when I did."

Children's book writer and illustrator Maurice Sendak was asked what he wanted children to get out of his books. He said, "I want them to know that we adults consider them heroes, living in such a difficult and cruel world."

It *is* a miracle for someone young to manage his or her way through youth. Maybe you are one of those living miracles, a young person on the verge of surviving your youth. If you have managed with God's help to steer around or plunge through the muck-holes of childhood, you have reason to rejoice.

Keep it up. Continue to pray for God's help as you make your life decisions and carry on toward your adulthood. Don't give in now. You are heroes and heroines.

---

*God our Creator, protect children from the horrors of life. Teach those who must face horrors to survive. I thank you for my survival. Help me to continue to survive and to overcome.*

---

# Integrity

"Do you still persist in your integrity? Curse God, and die."

JOB 2:9

The story of Job is a parable of a man caught between God and Satan. "Take away the goodies—the blessings and the wealth," Satan says to God, "—and *then* see if Job still loves you."

Unfair as it may seem, Satan is allowed to afflict Job in almost every way: Job loses family, flocks, even his health. God seems to have turned from him. "Give up your faith," his wife shouts. "Why bother?"

We sometimes feel like taking Mrs. Job's advice, forgetting our oh-so-lofty principles and just going to Hell in seven different ways: "Why maintain sexual integrity when all my friends are sleeping around?" "Why be honest when everyone in this office is stealing the company blind?" "Why be positive and friendly when everyone else seems to be into gossip and back stabbing?" "Why study when half this class will cheat?"

Ask yourself those questions ten years from now. Choosing integrity, like Job did—even at some cost to us—will be far more satisfying than the guilt, consequences, and downhill living of giving in.

Choosing right consistently gets easier, and running with the right crowd helps. Bad friends can pull you down. You and your good friends will hold each other up.

---

*Dear God, teach me, like Job, to keep my integrity and to make the good and faithful choices. Help me to accept the costs, or maybe to see them as part of the training—and the blessing.*

---

# Real Contentment

Keep your lives free from the love of money, and be content with
what you have.

HEBREWS 13:5

In his classic short story, *A Rocking Horse Winner*, D.H.
Lawrence tells a haunting story of a family whose house seems
to be saying, "There must be more money. There must be more
money." The haunting infuses young Paul, who gets on his
rocking horse and rocks and rocks until he mysteriously can
predict winners in the local horse races.

You will hear that voice many times in your life: "There must
be more money." You may also hear it as "get good grades," "get
into a good-paying profession," "work hard and get promoted,"
"be successful." Following these voices may tempt you to cut
corners, cheat, deceive, or walk all over co-workers or co-learners.

Jane Taylor, who wrote "Twinkle, Twinkle Little Star," also
wrote this:

One honest John Tompkins, a hedger and ditcher,
Although he was poor, did not want to be richer;
For all such vain wishes in him were prevented
By a fortunate habit of being contented.

Most of you won't be content to prune hedges and dig
ditches. Nevertheless "there is," as St. Paul once wrote to his
young friend Timothy, "great gain in godliness with
contentment" (1 Timothy 6:6).

Contentment may mean saying, "I have enough." Contentment
may mean learning that wealth and "things" bring no joy.

Godliness alone offers real contentment. Go for it.

---

*Dear Lord, give me contentment without laziness, ambition
without greed, and love of work without the love of money.*

---

# Fashion Me into Goodness

Women are raped in Zion, virgins in the towns of Judah.

LAMENTATIONS 5:11

Just being a man sometimes makes me ashamed. Men have exploited people, land, sea, and sky. As a political tool we have used famine, genocide, and war. I am haunted by images of Auschwitz and Buchenwald, by a photo of a black man chained to a tree and tortured to death with blowtorches. Is it any wonder that many women don't want their God to be pictured as a male figure?

The evil was in both Adam and Eve; both sinned, but we have not yet experienced a matriarchal society. Would women do better running the world? Would the corruption of power come as naturally to them as it came to us?

Rather than muse on evil, no matter what its gender, we would do better to team up—both men and women—to fight evil by emulating the good examples we have before us.

I have to keep telling myself that, yes, it is possible, under God, to be a good man. There have been many good examples. We start with Jesus himself, the man of all goodness. And then we can look at men of much goodness: St. John the evangelist of love, St. Francis, Lincoln, Schweitzer, Gandhi, Martin Luther King, Jr., and dozens more. There are men of much goodness that you and I know personally: teachers, pastors, my father, perhaps yours. Some young men reading this can already see goodness as one of their lives' goals and challenges.

The world can be less evil—but only if more good men and women are willing to step up and help run it.

---

*Lord God, fashion me more into goodness as Jesus was good.*

---

# An Unknown God

"I found among them an altar with the inscription, 'To an unknown god.' What therefore you worship as unknown, this I proclaim to you."

ACTS 17:23

The Greeks in ancient Athens worshipped many gods, and apparently—so as not to offend anyone—had raised an altar to an unknown god, just in case.

Paul took this just-in-case altar as a sermon illustration. "I'll tell you about this unknown God," he said to them, and proceeded to proclaim the Gospel of Jesus.

At moments in your life (maybe right now), your spiritual energy may be directed to an unknown God. You may have friends who reach out for an unknown God. God becomes unknown when the old pictures don't work anymore, when we can no longer believe in a grey-bearded old gentleman God in a rocking chair, or the buddy-buddy, walk-through-the-fields-together Jesus.

If, when you shut your spiritual eyes, you can see only an unknown God, then St. Paul has a message for you. "The God you worship as unknown, I make known to you," he says. "His name is Jesus of Nazareth."

Paul, a spiritually driven man, never saw Jesus in the flesh either. But Jesus came to Paul in a vision and made himself known.

If old, worn-out images have made Jesus an unknown stranger to you, go back to the roots of his truth, the Bible. Find the new Jesus who can speak to your new, more mature, more adult needs. He is there waiting for you, waiting to be known.

---

*Holy Spirit, wipe away the unknownness in my spiritual longings. Show me Jesus the God-man, my savior and my friend.*

# *Pushing Parents*

They should first learn their religious duty to their own family and make some repayment to their parents.

1 Timothy 5:4

Chapter 5 of Paul's first letter to Timothy deals with widows and orphans and a child's responsibility to parents and family. Yes, we do have a religious and moral duty to honor our parents and to do, so far as possible, what they expect and ask.

But some parents push. Some are far more than nudgers. Using the lever of financial support ("We pay your tuition, after all"), some parents would plan out our whole lives for us—often in ways that fulfill their *own* dreams rather than ours.

Actor Darryl Hickman once asked his mother, "Mom, how come I was out on the Hollywood set when I was only three years old?" Her answer? "Because that's what you always wanted to do."

That's funny, of course, and Darryl Hickman does not regret having a stage mom who pushed him into a career when he could barely walk, but many a doctor or lawyer or pastor who may secretly want to be a forest ranger or hairdresser may wish Mom or Dad hadn't pushed so hard.

We can be thankful that our parents have high hopes for us. They do know us, after all. They have raised us and studied us. We are their genetic product, and are apt to be more like them than we want to admit—and more apt to do as they did. But your parents' choice may not be either your choice or God's call—a message usually sent from within. Listen for that message; pray for it; study and talk with others who have heard it. Your parents may need to hear it—from you—as well.

---

*Lord, help me to see your path before me and to follow it into your service.*

---

# *Spiritual and Political*

"See, I am sending you out like sheep into the midst of wolves; so be wise as serpents and innocent as doves."

MATTHEW 10:16

Dietrich Bonhoeffer, the Christian martyr who died in a Nazi concentration camp, wrote:

The more spiritual you are, the more political you are. Only if you cry for the Jews, can you sing Gregorian Chant.

Even by themselves those are wise and powerful words. But they gain more power when we know something about Bonhoeffer. A professor of New Testament theology at the University of Berlin in the 1930s, he urged Christians to social involvement and organized the Pastors' Emergency League against the Nazis. Arrested by the Gestapo in 1943, he was hanged after the 1944 plot to assassinate Hitler.

We listen carefully to martyrs such as Bonhoeffer. People die for the wrong causes, of course—witness Jonestown and the Branch Davidians—but when Bonhoeffer reminds us that beautiful church music doesn't alleviate human suffering, we weigh his truth against his sacrificial death.

Keeping church and state separate doesn't mean Christians should be politically neutral. Only if those with faith and vision stay involved and keep the pressure on will our government work for justice, world peace, and the easing of suffering. When Jesus asked, "When did we see thee hungry, or thirsty, or a stranger, or sick, or imprisoned?" (Matthew 25:31-46), he was challenging his followers to lives of concern about the needs of others. We pass part—but not all—of that challenge along to those we elect to govern us.

---

*Empower me, Holy Spirit, to be more actively involved in the human condition.*

---

# Help My Unbelief

"You of little faith, why did you doubt?"

MATTHEW 14:31

L ord," Peter said, "if it is you, bid me come to you on the water." He walked on water, and through a storm. A miracle. Peter walked on water until he doubted—then he sank.

Maybe sometimes when your faith wavers, you are trying something that seems just as impossible as walking on water. Maybe you also face your challenge under stormy or difficult conditions. Away from home, you don't have the support systems you once had either. You may be walking on eggs or up to your knees in muck. The miracle is that things don't break up worse than they do or get stickier than they are.

Doubts creep in. Fear of failure; fear that God will not sustain you now, as you were once sustained; fear that God won't approve or won't listen to your prayers; fear that you will sink. Perhaps you even fear—oh misery!—that God isn't even there, and that the whole Jesus business is somebody's dreamed-up story.

Peter took his eyes off Jesus. That's why he sank. He lost his focus. That's where our fears come from, that's why the storm sweeps in, that's why we sink. We take our eyes off Jesus.

But Jesus' promise is there, and it is good: Peter walked on water. We might not need to walk on water, but if handling relationships, facing substance abuse, or making other important changes or choices seem impossible, remember: with our eyes on Jesus, we can do almost anything.

---

L ord, I believe; help my unbelief.

---

# The Power of Evil

"Deliver us from evil."

MATTHEW 6:13 (KJV)

Two ten-year-old boys abduct a three-year-old from a shopping center, take him to a deserted railroad yard, beat and torture him to death, then leave his body on a railroad track to be cut in half. Why? Where do such atrocities come from? They are the power of evil unleashed in the world. They are Satan dwelling in human beings, taking them over, and making them the embodiment of evil. "Deliver us from such evil."

That same evil (Shudder, shudder!) is in each of us. The best of us is capable of the worst kinds of evil under pressure of some unforeseen temptation or extremity. "Deliver *me* from evil deeds."

Focusing only on evil can terrify and paralyze us. We then begin to see the world as a hopelessly evil place. It is not. Evil and sin are in the world, but so is God. God is good. God promises to be with us always, even through the valley of the shadow, even to the end of the age. "Deliver me from evil."

---

*Lord, the kingdom and the power and the glory are yours—and so is the world—now and forever. Never let me forget that.*

---

# God's Garden

The Lord God planted a garden in Eden . . . and there he put the man whom he had formed. Out of the ground the Lord God made to grow every tree that is pleasant to the sight and good for food.

GENESIS 2:8-9

Eden's paradise was portrayed as a garden. Adam and Eve were invited to stroll and enjoy. Life was easy. Work was unheard of.

Gardens are still places of quiet refuge, of contemplative strolls, and of pleasant puttering. But making and keeping them that way is a lot of work.

Most of God's world today is no garden. The world has been pillaged, ravaged, and polluted almost beyond reclaiming. In more and more places, our once-productive soil has lost all its nutrients. Lakes and rivers are dying. Forests are cut down, cut up; the slash is burned. Crops are planted and animals grazed in impossible places. Wetlands are drained, dry lands flooded. Even the endless sea and the air have become garbage dumps.

The Bible's command to humankind was to "subdue" the earth, which may have meant to understand the world and let it serve our needs. "Subduing" has since come to be a dirty word, an invitation to human greed and exploitation.

You and your children will have to become God's gardeners once again—but no longer by subduing. "Nurturing" is better, "cherishing" better than that. And with all God's other wonderful and useful creatures, "co-existing."

---

*Teach me, Lord, to walk in this world, your fragile garden, with renewed reverence.*

---

# The Debt We Owe

> But that same slave, as he went out, came upon one of his fellow slaves who owed him a hundred denarii; and seizing him by the throat, he said, "Pay what you owe."
>
> MATTHEW 18:28

One slave in Jesus' parable is forgiven a debt of ten thousand talents ($15 million). He then turns around and refuses to forgive a fellow slave one hundred denarii ($25).

How does the first slave get into such debt? It is beyond our imagination, not to mention his earning power. Unless he won the powerball lottery, no one would bother suing a nearly penniless servant for $15 million. He could neither incur nor pay such a debt.

This is a spiritual story.

The debt we owe God is ten thousand talents, and more—an incredible ledger full. We owe God everything—for life, health, care and watchfulness, forgiveness, everything—beyond what even our imaginations could dream up. God has given us everything, forgiven us everything.

Having been given and forgiven so much puts us in a more giving and forgiving frame of mind toward Mom or Dad or Bubba or Sis or a neighbor or a "former" friend. How could we not forgive that little 25-buck sin or oversight or wrong?

In the light of God's great love for us, the little forgivenesses and loves and restorations we make with those around us come more naturally and seem a pittance.

---

*Make me, my forgiving God and Lord, more forgiving of those around me. Melt down my ancient grudges and old scores in the warmth of your gracious love.*

---

# True Friends

"I do not call you servants any longer ... but I have called you friends."

JOHN 15:15

In John 15, the friendship chapter, Jesus shares important truths with his disciples. They now know not only his teachings, but also his mission on earth and his impending passion: he makes them one with him and calls them friends.

Jesus and his disciples became deeper friends when they shared deeper truths. Jesus had almost a dozen such friends—three of them extra special: Peter, James, and John.

You and I probably have a dozen friends too, and several of them extra special.

Our closest friends will be like Jesus' inner circle of disciples. We will be with them at special times, tell them special things, and expect much of them. We share with such friends our deepest thoughts. They are far more important than "Hi-there," or "Let's-go-do-something-fun," or "double-date" friends.

You go to such a friend when you need to tell someone, "I'm going to be married," or "My brother just told me he's gay," or "I feel like killing myself." Such friends come to us with similar messages. We tell each other almost everything. Almost.

The only friend that we can tell *absolutely* everything is our friend Jesus himself. He is absolutely faithful and loves us just as we are.

---

*Lord Jesus, you are my best friend. Give me other good friends, and show me how to value and keep them. Help me also to be a true friend to them.*

---

# Equal Pay

They grumbled against the landowner, saying, "These last worked only one hour, and you have made them equal to us who have borne the burden of the day and the scorching heat."

MATTHEW 20:11-12

Jesus' parable of the wages says that we all get the same from God, whether we have been lifetime saints or, like the thief on the cross, repent at the last minute.

Life, however, is different. There is little "justice" in the way labor, commitment, faithfulness, loyalty, and productivity are rewarded. Missionaries earn less than big city clergy. Inner-city or small-town teachers may earn less than those in the suburbs, even though they may work harder.

Actress Greta Garbo, although the bigger star, left for Sweden in the middle of a film because John Gilbert, her leading man, was getting $10,000 a week and she only $600.

There is no equality. John the Baptist exhorted hearers to be generous with the poor, tax collectors to be honest, soldiers not to resort to extortion or theft. "Be content with your wages," he said (Luke 3:10-14).

It's hard to choose a life of service and watch our friends getting double and triple and quadruple our salaries. It's hard to do God's work for an entire lifetime and retire with next to nothing. Or is it nothing?

Earthly rewards are only that. "Lay up for yourselves treasures in heaven," Jesus once said. Who can measure the usefulness and good in a lifetime of service?

---

Lord, show me my calling and help me to go for it without looking back in envy or discontent.

---

# *Righteous Indignation*

[Jesus] entered the temple and began to drive out those who were selling and those were buying in the temple, and he overturned the tables of the money changers and the seats of those who sold doves.

If we ever have any doubts that Jesus was truly human, we need only go back and study the account of his anger and frustration in the temple. Righteous indignation, you could call it. Worship and God were so important to Jesus that he couldn't bear to see the temple desecrated. He wanted those who worshipped to have the best of motives and to practice the most spiritual of religious exercises. Unfortunately, the temple looked more like a cross between an auction and a casino. And it made him angry.

Our own righteous indignation sometimes comes from smaller causes, from more shaky foundations. When we lay our righteous indignation on friends and families, boyfriends and girlfriends, we are saying that they have disappointed or failed us. Our anger isn't necessarily righteous, even if we turn over tables and kick over chairs.

At such times we need to look in a mirror. Is that the face of Christ? Who am I to tell anyone else how to act? Who appointed me Mr. Perfect, Ms. Perfect, the judge of others' behavior?

It's one thing for Jesus to smash his way through the temple: he was and is, after all, the Son of God. But where do I get off being uppity and indignant? Who gives me the right? What special class was I born into?

---

*Slap me down when I get "righteously indignant," Holy Spirit. Show me also Jesus on his knees, washing the feet of his friends.*

---

# The Gift of Life

Whatever is true, whatever is honorable, whatever is just, whatever is pure, whatever is pleasing, whatever is commendable, if there is any excellence and if there is anything worthy of praise, think about these things.

PHILIPPIANS 4:8

Most young people entertain suicidal thoughts at one time or another. Feeling depressed, they may believe that the world would be better off without them. They are wrong.

Remember the ever-popular Christmas film, *It's a Wonderful Life*? An angel named Clarence takes control of time and rebuilds a small community as it might have been if George (the main character, played by Jimmy Stewart) had never lived. It is a harsher, more evil town. George's wife is an unhappy spinster. The brother he saved from drowning *did* drown. George saw how many other lives his life had touched. "You've been given a great gift, George," Clarence says, "to see what the world would have been like without you."

Paul reminds us in Philippians that much in life is just and pure and gracious and excellent. Some of that good lies ahead of you, some of it you will be responsible for. An angel Clarence, perhaps in the guise of a friend or pastor or teacher—can show you that good.

Sometimes you yourself are asked to be the angel Clarence for a depressed friend. It's scary, but pray—and be positive—about life and hope and tomorrow.

I expect most potential suicides, if they could envision the future with themselves in it, would never dream of giving up their lives so soon and so selfishly and so foolishly.

---

*Spirit of comfort, companion of my soul, pull me out of my dark holes when I slip into them, and help me to pull others out of theirs. Send many Clarences to teach us ever to see life as important, gracious, excellent, and beautiful.*

---

# Gifts and Calling

I therefore, the prisoner in the Lord, beg you to lead a life worthy
of the calling to which you have been called.

EPHESIANS 4:1

In these words to the Ephesian church, St. Paul also reminds
me that I am called to be a Christian. But is that my only
vocation? What else does God call me to be?

I once wrote a book, now out of print, called *What Does God
Want Me to Do with My Life?* A lot of people bought that book
because of the title. We *do* want to know God's will for our lives.
Wouldn't we be thrilled to hear God say: "Be a pastor." "Be a
youth worker." "Be a mechanic." "Be a nurse."

Most of us will hear the voice of God in more veiled ways. We
may go for long periods without ever being sure that we are
doing what God wants. We needn't worry. God is there, guiding
us. As I get to the far side of my working life, I can look back
and see God's hand in many of my choices, in many doors that
were shut in my face, in both disappointments and achievements.

You will learn that vocational choices usually move alongside
of gifts, and we all have gifts: people gifts, organizational gifts,
hand and eye skills, intuitions. Take an hour sometime, and sort
through your gifts. List them. Rejoice in them. Then share your
list with friends and family and counselors—people who know
you. Ask them what you might be good at. God opens some
doors and closes others on the basis of the talents and gifts he
has given us.

"Where your talent and the world's needs come together,"
Aristotle said long ago, "therein lies your vocation."

---

*Creator Lord, you gave me gifts. Teach me to sort them out and
to use them to serve you as I fulfill my life's callings.*

---

# Endangered Species

You make springs gush forth in the valleys. . . . giving drink to every wild animal. . . . By the streams the birds of the air have their habitation. . . . the earth is satisfied with the fruit of your work.

PSALM 104:10-13

God's nature, left to itself, will remain beautiful, will never destroy itself nor create ugliness.

Humankind alone creates a greedy ugliness. We build mansions on fragile hillsides and row houses on fertile plains. Our factories pollute air and water. We strip the earth for minerals and drill its skin for oil and irrigation. Everywhere we pollute and despoil.

The animals are the first to notice our pollution and destruction. So are those who live close to the earth. "Whatever happens to the beast," Chief Seattle once said, "soon happens to humankind. All things are connected."

If Chief Seattle is right, then, unless we humans change our ways, *we* are the endangered species.

Many children are catching on. They are consuming less, recycling, and learning to care for the earth. Can they teach my older generation anything?

You who are in the middle will have to make hard choices. Will you exploit and consume as we older Americans have? Or will you learn earth care, as your kid sisters and brothers are doing?

---

*Creator Lord, forgive us for spoiling your beautiful earth. Teach us to do better and to live more in harmony with the beasts and the birds.*

---

# Guilt!

Wash me thoroughly from my iniquity, and cleanse me from my sin.

PSALM 51:2

When King David writes, "Thou forgavest the iniquity of my sin," he is most likely referring to guilt.

Guilt troubles many of us. We may try to accept God's forgiveness, but our rotten, nagging guilt doesn't go away.

We can "make up" for our sins: make amends with acts of goodness or by compensating or paying back those we have hurt—at least by apologizing. But sometimes we're still left with the guilt.

We *have* hurt people—family, friends, girlfriends, boyfriends. We have hurt ourselves and others, repeatedly breaking God's laws by our deceit, theft, gossip, fornication, doubt, by laying seige to our own bodies with alcohol and drugs. Guilt. You can make your list of its causes; I can make mine.

God also forgives guilt. Our iniquity—our guilt—can be thoroughly washed away, a mental springtime, a clean slate. When Jesus forgave an adulterous woman and saved her from stoning, he said: "Go and sin no more."

It must grieve God something awful to wash us over and over, and then watch us jump back in the same muck hole. Some sins are compulsive, of course, and will require counseling and treatment to overcome; but prayer and plain old willpower can conquer most of them.

---

*Holy Spirit, help me to root out my pet sins, the sins that cause me guilt and grieve God because I do them over and over. Give me strength to face them and power to overcome them.*

---

# A Sharp Tongue

> But now you must get rid of all such things—anger, wrath, malice, slander, and abusive language from your mouth.

COLOSSIANS 3:8

Living in close quarters with others, working closely with others, getting to know others' habits and ways, can lead to sins of the mouth, some of which Paul lists above. When we are bored or miffed or jealous—or sometimes for no good reason at all—we badmouth others, gossiping about them, pointing out their faults and shortcomings, passing on stories that are unkind, perhaps even untrue.

One of the commandments Moses brought down from the mountain was aimed at our mouths: "Don't bear false witness." We need to be reminded of that commandment every day, since our mouths are so apt to get us into trouble.

Washington Irving, the early American writer of *The Legend of Sleepy Hollow,* once wrote, "A sharp tongue is the only tool that grows keener with constant use."

We often sharpen our tongues on others in order to feel better about ourselves, to ease our own feelings of inferiority. This never works. Deep down, gossip and slander make us feel even worse about ourselves. Martin Luther's explanation of the Eighth Commandment teaches us a better way to speak of our friends and neighbors: "Defend them, speak well of them, and explain their actions in the kindest way."

---

*Holy Spirit, teach me neighborliness. Show me more and more how to think kind thoughts and to say kind things of others.*

---

# *Brothers and Sisters*

And when they were in the field, Cain rose up against his brother Abel, and killed him.

GENESIS 4:8

Only four chapters into the Bible, humanity's religious history—we haven't even gotten past the first generation of people—and already one brother has killed another.

Holocaust survivor Elie Wiesel says, "One hates his brother better. That's why civil war is the worst of all wars."

That's also why family feuds are often so bitter and so long-lasting. We naturally expect the best from our own kith and kin; we are ever so much more disappointed when they seem to let us down.

Leaving home, as you are doing, is a break point. When a sibling moves out on his or her own, a gap is created. Things look different from across that gap. Your brother or sister, who seemed forever to have been your worst enemy, can gradually become one of your trusted friends. Now that you no longer live in the same house and compete for the same space, the same attention, and the same affection, things can and should be better.

If there were problems with your siblings, you can hasten things along with a phone call or a letter. Apologize. Make an overture. Reach out. Accept some of the blame. Invite your sister out for breakfast. Cain and Abel represent the worst kind of sibling rivalry. God can help us also reach for the *best* in ourselves—love, forgiveness, sharing, caring. Moving out on our own gives us a fresh new chance.

---

*Dear God, creator of families, teach me to love my family more now that I am away from it—and especially my siblings.*

---

# Saints and Sinners

"Truly I tell you, the tax collectors and the prostitutes go into the kingdom of God ahead of you."

A few of you who are reading this might be in danger of spiritual pride. This one is for you. Your profile might be something like this: nicest kid in your graduating class, clean-living, never rebelled, a regular in church, constant in prayer. But do you sometimes look at others and wonder how they can choose wrong so often, be so depraved, so sinful?

Jesus dealt with almost every kind of sin and human misery. He found spiritual pride the hardest to stomach. The spiritually proud became his enemies, and finally his killers. They harassed him, shadowed and spied on him, needled him with hard questions, and constantly accused him of consorting with ne'er-do-wells and sinners.

He *did* consort with sinners—people who knew they were sinners and knew they needed Jesus' forgiveness. "Those who are well," he once said, "have no need of a physician, but those who are sick; I have not come to call the righteous, but sinners to repentance" (Luke 5:31-32).

Take another look at the sinners around you. Novelist Flannery O'Conner wrote: "We often learn more about God from misfits than from do-gooders or saints."

The spiritually proud think they are doing it right: living the good life, believing the right truths, and holding to and demanding of others proper moral choices. Jesus tends to see that attitude as a blindness.

---

*R*oot out my pride, gentle Savior. Forgive and restore me to gracious humility and to active service.

---

# The Beauty of the World

> I have seen the business that God has given to everyone to be busy with. He has made everything suitable for its time; moreover he has put a sense of past and future into their minds.

ECCLESIASTES 3:10-11

There is so much to do, so much to learn. Wherever we study or live or work, there is natural beauty to explore: mountains, hills, forests, rivers, lakes, the sea. Beauty is also expressed in the arts: music, drama, sculpture, painting, film. So much to see, so much to experience.

Experiencing the beauty of nature and the beauty that can be created by human beings puts eternity into our minds. We marvel at the richness of creation and the possibilities borne in the human spirit and the human mind. It is like Shakespeare's Hamlet says of the human creature:

> What a piece of work is man, how noble in reason, how infinite in faculties, in form and moving, how express and admirable, in action, how like an angel, in apprehension, how like a god! The beauty of the world; the paragon of animals ...

Becoming more aware of the beauty and variety of God's natural creation reminds us of the beauty and variety and potential in humankind—all of us, creatures of God. The more we study nature and art, the more we should learn reverence for life, especially human life. The God who made us so beautifully creative, and made a world so beautiful for our dwelling, wants us to live together in peace, to deal with each other in justice, and to help one another in loving service.

---

*Show me, Creator God, the stamp of your creative hand, not only in the beauty of nature, but in the creativity of your creatures.*

---

# Risk Management

"If one blind person leads another, both will fall into a pit."

MATTHEW 15:14

We take risks all of our lives. Most of the life-threatening risks, though—the absolutely crazy things—we do when we are young. Young men, especially, are often foolish risk-takers—recklessly jumping, diving, climbing, driving—especially when they are in groups. They are sometimes killed or injured for life. Alcohol and drugs massively multiply these risks.

There are so many kinds of risks that we *have* to take, and we need to fail from time to time, but not at the foolish expense of life or limb or future or reputation. Circus performers have safety nets; young risk-takers don't.

Our younger years are designed for failure. We have little experience and many opportunities to start over.

Some risks, however, offer no second chance. Dive in water that is too shallow and you may be in a wheelchair the rest of your life. Drive too dangerously and you may not even live to be in a wheelchair. Your foolishness may hurt or kill not only yourself and your best friends, but innocent strangers.

Caring friends can often help you with risk management. They can help keep you in a safe place. They will not let you do what is dangerously dumb, but will watch and enjoy your safer experiments, picking you up and brushing you off after failures.

Remember that your risk management is also monitored by the Holy Spirit and your guardian angel and, if you are so blessed, by loved ones who pray for you each day.

---

*Lord, help me to fail safely—and to learn from my failures.*

---

# Guiding Spirit

O sing to the Lord a new song.

PSALM 98:1

Kathleen Battle, renowned singer, was also very good in mathematics and chose it as her college major. Her vocal teacher had talked her into studying music; but on her way to college, she remembered good grades in math, and thought how much easier it would be to make a living with math training than with music training. She decided to become a math major.

At college, when she went to register, the line of students waiting to sign up for the sciences was *very* long. She glanced over at the music registration desk: hardly anyone.

She went to the shorter line, signed up, and her life's work began.

Is it really luck or chance? A line is too long, so we change our major. We get stuck in traffic and miss one job opportunity but get another. We meet a missionary or a teacher or a businesswoman who gives us a vision of a life's work.

My wife and I had been on the same small campus for a whole year and had not noticed each other. Two weeks before I graduated, we met at a lake ten miles out of town. Chance? Maybe, but I say God put us there, where we would *have* to notice each other.

Be aware that some things that happen may not be chance at all. Look for God's hand in your "chance" encounters, opportunities, and experiences. Looking back, you will see that hand guiding you.

---

*Guiding Spirit, show me persons I should meet, places I should see, opportunities I should have—and keep me wide awake while you are doing it.*

---

# Simple Gifts

"Look at the birds of the air; they neither sow nor reap nor gather together into barns, and yet your heavenly Father feeds them. Are you not of more value than they?"

MATTHEW 6:26

While traveling on government business in Europe, former Minnesota Governor Albert Quie saw a medical apparatus in a druggist's shop that pulled him up short. He picked up and examined a small bristle brush with two suction cups attached to it. He bought it and took it home to his father.

Home on the farm, the elder Mr. Quie knew right away what the brush was for. He headed for the bathroom; Al followed. Mr. Quie wet the brush and the suction cups, attached the brush to the wall of the sink, soaped it, and demonstrated—with tears running down his cheeks—how he could now scrub his hand without help. Mr. Quie had lost an arm in a farm accident years earlier.

A simple gift.

Sometimes we appreciate least the simple, uncomplicated things that are best. How often do we give thanks for the simplest things God gives us? Two hands that can be used to wash each other. Two feet that walk us around. Two eyes to judge perspective and distance. Two ears to sense a sound's direction. A family. Friends. A home town. A church. A job.

So often we long for and work for and tell ourselves we need expensive, esoteric, and complicated things. Jesus reminds us of the birds of the air and tells us not to worry.

---

*Dear Lord, make us content with what we have. Teach us to look at the simple gifts that are ours—life, health, love, friends, and family.*

---

# Dreams and Visions

Your young men shall see visions, and your old men shall dream dreams.

ACTS 2:17

Idealism and youth go together. Optimism and youth go together. If neglect or abuse don't altogether drive it out, most young people survive their teen years and still have a lot of hope. They see a future ahead of them that glows, that shines. They believe there is nothing they can't do if they work hard and apply themselves.

Life, at some point, begins to hack notches in those attitudes. Writer Joan Didion records one of hers:

> The day that I did not make Phi Beta Kappa ... marked the end of something. ... I lost the conviction that lights would always turn green for me.

Most of us haven't had or will not have a chance to be turned down by Phi Beta Kappa, the most prestigious of academic honor societies. But we will all have some important door shut in our faces. We will not make the team; we will not get the job; we will not get into the college or graduate school of our choice. We will be turned down by the guy or gal of our dreams.

Life is full of disappointments, large and small. The older we get, the less idealistic we become. Those older people we enjoy the most, though, are the ones who still have *some* of the optimism and idealism of youth. A lot of them are people of faith. Because they know God in Christ, they always have an open door that makes even large disappointments seem small.

---

*Lord God, I know your world is a hard place, but keep me from being beaten down by it. Keep me living toward a bright tomorrow.*

---

# Gentle Witness

> Saul, still breathing threats and murder against the disciples of the Lord went to the high priest and asked him for letters to the synagogues at Damascus, so that if he found any who belonged to the Way, men or women, he might bring them bound to Jerusalem.
>
> ACTS 9:1-2

Saul was driven by an intense religious prejudice. He believed his faith to be the only religious truth. The teachings of Jesus, therefore, and those who followed those teachings, were seen as enemies of his own religious truth.

Religious prejudice fuels some of the world's worst cruelties and evils. Early Christians were persecuted relentlessly, from Saul on through several centuries under cruel pagan Roman emperors. First-century historian Tacitus writes:

> Christians were covered in the skins of wild animals and then torn to death by dogs, or crucified, or set on fire. They burned like torches in the night. Nero opened up his own garden for this spectacle, and gave a show in the arena.

Religious prejudice still fuels animosities and bloodshed in Northern Ireland, the former Yugoslavia, the Middle East, Central America, Canada—and in the United States.

Away from your home and neighborhood and church, you will encounter different religious beliefs. This book has encouraged you to hold to your family faith. That should not, however, include hatred and intolerance and violence toward those who do not share those beliefs. Jesus was a man of peace and love. Only with such tools can we persuade others to join our ranks.

---

*Lord Jesus, king of peace and love, root out my prejudices and make me a gentle witness.*

---

# Overcoming Evil

Beloved, never avenge yourselves, but leave room for the wrath of God; for it is written, "Vengeance is mine, I will repay, says the Lord."

ROMANS 12:19

Sweet revenge," it is called—the deep satisfaction of getting even, of paying someone back for a slight, a hurt, or an evil deed. Especially when we are young, we lie awake brooding, plotting, dreaming of getting even. People out there have hurt us and hurt us bad; and we want to pay them back.

Many old systems of justice before Jesus' time were built on hurt for hurt. You can read about one of them in the Old Testament book of Leviticus:

When someone causes a disfigurement in a neighbor, as he has done, it shall be done to him, fracture for fracture, eye for eye, tooth for tooth.

Gandhi had a different idea: "An eye for an eye only makes the world blind."

It is hard to swallow the hurt, but it can be done. Meditating on Christ's words, "Father forgive them," can help. Hardened criminals are sometimes so touched by the forgiveness and love in their victims that their lives are changed.

Revenge may be sweet, but forgiveness and love are sweeter—and certainly better for society. Jesus himself taught it: "Love your enemies, and pray for those who persecute you" (Matthew 5:44). The writer of Romans also picks it up: "If your enemy is hungry, feed him; if he is thirsty, give him drink. . . . Do not be overcome by evil, but overcome evil with good" (Romans 12:20-21).

---

*Quench my desire for revenge, gentle Lord, with waves of your love. Teach me to overcome evil with good.*

---

# Hidden Self

But who can detect their errors? Clear me from hidden faults.

PSALM 19:12

Much of the time, we can't see our own faults. We all have little glitches, annoying habits that may have seemed more normal in our home neighborhoods or with our own families. Now that we live away from home, however, and spend so much time with people we don't know very well, the glitches may be bothering others.

The human species is endlessly interesting. Friends who are absolutely faultless are usually absolutely dull. So we cherish embarrassing but harmless glitches—like telling loud jokes in restaurants. Writer Clifton Fadiman wrote, "I am lucky in my friends, for they, like me, are rich in faults." He went on to say that seeing those faults in each other, and enjoying their irony, was a part of the friendship.

But how should we react to more harmful habits—like profanity, or shoplifting, or sneaking into games and films without paying, or shady sexual attitudes and practices?

In Shakespeare's *King Henry IV,* Prince Hal enjoyed the faults and foibles in Falstaff until Hal became king; then he absolutely rejected both Falstaff and their youthful foolishness.

When free spending becomes wastefulness, when joy in good food becomes gluttony, when drinking becomes drunkenness, when chit-chat becomes gossip—it's time to take a serious look.

---

*Show me, Lord, my hidden self. Help me to root out that which grieves you and others.*

---

# An Instrument of Justice

"Do not be afraid, little flock, for it is your Father's good pleasure
to give you the kingdom."

LUKE 12:32

To begin with, those who fought racial prejudice in this
country were a little flock. They have not yet inherited the
kingdom. We are a long way from dealing fully and honestly
with racial prejudice; but great advances in awareness have been
made, and in just my lifetime. Black track star Jesse Owens was
a first. He won four Olympic gold medals in 1936, tweaking
Hitler's doctrine of Aryan superiority. A decade later, in 1947,
Jackie Robinson began playing baseball for the Brooklyn
Dodgers. He was not easily or quickly accepted—blacks had
their own leagues back then—but he became a baseball legend.

Now hundreds of blacks dominate many professional sports.
In some sports, whites are the exception.

There are still far too many racial tensions in our world. Wars
of racial hatred rage across Europe and Africa and on our own
urban streets. But doors have been opened. Mal Good, the first
black TV newscaster, said,

> In the early days I wouldn't have been allowed to stay in the William
> Penn Hotel. I have lived long enough to have been invited to speak
> in their ballroom.

Only as we all work steadily, faithfully, and tirelessly, can we
make our society work better. Especially important are people
like you, young people of goodwill, who will devote yourselves
to making it happen.

---

*Lord Jesus, first root out prejudice in my own heart, then make
me an instrument of justice and goodwill.*

---

# Pray Wisely

Rejoice always, pray without ceasing, give thanks in all circumstances.

1 THESSALONIANS 5:16-18

For years, playwright George Bernard Shaw kept up a lively correspondence with a nun, Dame Laurentia McLachlan. Shaw, an outspoken old curmudgeon—and certainly no saint—was touched to know that Sister McLachlan prayed for him. He once wrote her:

> You'll go on praying for me, won't you, no matter how surprising the results might be?

There are probably people who pray regularly for you. Do they tell you they are doing it? Do you pray for others? Do you tell them? Some people wouldn't understand; but for those who would—or for those who may not know we care enough to pray for them—it is often worth letting them know.

When I have told people that I will pray for them, they usually say a simple thank you. I have never had anyone say, "Don't you dare," or "What right do you have to pray for me?"

Occasionally someone will say, "I'm not sure if it will do any good." I usually answer, "I'm pretty sure it will—that's why I do it." Praying for others keeps them on my mind, and makes me more concerned. Sometimes my prayers lead me to be active in someone's life. Thus, God uses me as part of the answer to my own prayer.

Pray for your family, your friends, and those you know are in need. And tell them you are praying for them. Listen for God's suggestions, too. It will be good for them *and* for you.

---

*Lord God, teach me to pray wisely. Show me those who need my prayers, and give me the courage to tell them they are being lifted up before you in prayer.*

---

# From Mourning into Morning

Solid food is for the mature, for those whose faculties have been trained by practice to distinguish good from evil.

HEBREWS 5:14

When the worst happens, how can we believe in a loving, caring God?

Pioneer novelist Ole Rolvaag's daughter Ella remembers the day her little brother drowned after falling through the rotten wooden ceiling of a neighbor's backyard cistern. Little five-year-old Paul Gunnar, pulling a red wagon, had cut through the same neighbor's backyard dozens of times before. Why did the cistern cave in on that day? Why did it not collapse under the weight of some adult who would have been tall enough to stand in the bottom, head above water, and shout for help?

"We all slept in the same bed that night," Ella said, "and looked at the stars. Father tried to fit my little brother's senseless drowning into his faith in a merciful God."

Senseless accidents and deadly diseases wipe away not only innocent children, but friends and family. Who can understand pain and suffering and evil in the world?

It is not God's will that innocent children suffer or that anyone be cursed with evil. On the contrary, God is our most constant comforter who never leaves or forsakes us. Friends and family will comfort us, but only the peace of God can, as poet George Barker says, move us "from mourning into morning."

---

*Gentle Spirit, show us a loving, caring God who weeps with us at pain and suffering, a God whose own Son also suffered and died because of the world's evil powers.*

---

# Made Clean

"Be perfect, therefore, as your heavenly Father is perfect."

MATTHEW 5:48

The dove doesn't come down to a dirty perch," says Robert Shaw, director of the world-famous Robert Shaw Chorale. When you want the result to be divine, he explains, you have to keep everything clean: pitch, tone, enunciation—everything.

In Christ's scheme of things, however, the Dove (the Holy Spirit) *does* come down to a dirty perch. What other sort of perch could we possibly offer to a perfect, spiritual visitor? The minute that Dove lands, though, the perch is cleansed, sterilized, immaculate.

The incredible stumbling block of the Christian faith is that Christ *does* come to us, just as we are. We are pulled out of the septic tank of our sins and washed up squeaky clean.

The fourth work of the Holy Spirit, according to Martin Luther's wonderful *Small Catechism,* is to sanctify us, to make us into saints—holy, more Christ-like.

To begin with we are declared holy, like being granted knighthood or citizenship by a king or a judge. Over time we are taught and enabled to live our lives in more holiness.

There is no amount of effort we could expend, no list of good works we could do, to earn or attain such holiness. When we trust in God through Christ we are *declared* holy: a gift.

Our response is thanksgiving.

---

*Holy Spirit, Dove divine, strengthen my faith and continue to show me paths of holiness. Give me saints to emulate and truths to follow.*

---

# Gradual Paths

"Which of you, intending to build a tower, does not first sit down and
estimate the cost, to see whether he has enough to complete it?"

LUKE 14:28

Dreams of a rich and fulfilling future fuel our youth. We
want to get there and stay there. Moving too fast too soon,
though, can be risky. I watch some of our graduates get high-
salaried, corporate jobs right out of college; and just when they
are beginning to feel secure and very good about themselves, the
corporations decide to cut back, leaving the low-rungers staring
at their mortgages and car payments.

Per Hansa, the hero of Ole Rolvaag's prairie saga, *Giants in
the Earth,* tells his rival Torkal Tallakson, "It's better to begin in
a gopher hole than to end in one."

Instead of building a sod hut like the other farmers, Tallakson
plans on building a large frame house right away. Hansa tells
him he should use the house money to buy horses and cattle and
machinery and to hire extra hands to help him farm. "Then in a
few years," Hansa says, "you'd be king of us all."

I expect most of us would like to start at the top, even though
we have invested no time in getting needed experience. But
experience is the horsepower that makes employees valuable
and can pull them through hard times. Getting experience is
often what it will cost to build your dream. Failing is a learning
experience, we are told, but it is much safer to fail in small ways,
learning on the way up. It's a long fall when we fail at the top of
the ladder.

---

*Lord Jesus, king of the humble, show me gradual paths to a life
of service and satisfaction.*

---

# The Beginning of Wisdom

God looks down from heaven on humankind to see if there are any who are wise, who seek after God.

PSALM 53:2

The psalmist says that those who seek after God are wise. Do you agree? Do people you know or work with or study with think the Godly are wise?

Elsewhere the psalmist writes, "The fear of the Lord is the beginning of wisdom."

Following God may not always seem wise, nor will being godly always seem to lead to the wisest courses of action. But taking the long view, the Psalmist has it right. Seeking after God is finally believing in God, relating to God. In that relationship God teaches us to value truth, openness, the welfare of others, uprightness, morality, and a dozen other abstract qualities we could list.

But in action these qualities are not abstract. If we see someone stealing or cheating or injuring or abusing or even belittling someone else, we have to act, because we are filled with God's wisdom.

There are consequences for our actions. Those we thought were our friends will sometimes turn from us when we stand up for what we believe to be right and godly. We may lose a job or a vocational opportunity. You will never regret choosing right, however, because that is choosing God. Dozens of people—you can see them on TV and read about them in the news—regret not standing up for truth, justice, and righteousness when they had a chance.

*Dear God, show me your ways clearly, and give me the courage to follow them, regardless of the consequences.*

# A Way of Escape

God is faithful, and he will not let you be tested beyond your strength, but with the testing he will also provide the way out so that you may be able to endure it.

1 CORINTHIANS 10:13

God is faithful. What a great truth to write on the palms of our hands and on the bottoms of our feet before we reach out or hike off.

I suppose when we really feel our spiritual dynamos purring, we think we can face any temptation. "What, me do drugs? No way. Heck, if all my friends were doing drugs and I could get all the stuff I wanted free, I wouldn't."

Maybe so. Maybe so. But we ought not presume on the power of God or the strength of our own faith. God may allow me to be tempted and may provide the way of escape, but what if I myself wade into pools of temptation? What if I tempt God by taking foolhardy risks, and my faith cannot keep me from drowning?

It pays to choose good friends and follow wholesome paths. We may think we are strong enough to face any temptation; we may think we will be the strong ones in a friendship or relationship with someone who has problems. It isn't always that easy.

Yes, God is faithful. But God also let us be born with brains. To risk making a mess out of our lives by walking heedlessly through any old valley of the shadow of death is just asking for it.

---

*Dear Lord, my strength and protector, I know you will not lead me into temptation. Keep others from doing that, too. When temptation cannot be avoided, I claim your promise to show me a way of escape.*

---

# Hosts of Angels

> The Spirit immediately drove [Jesus] out into the wilderness. He was in the wilderness forty days, tempted by Satan; and he was with the wild beasts; the angels waited on him.
>
> MARK 1:12-13

We, too, live in a wilderness. We, too, are tempted by Satan. We, too, seem to be surrounded by wild animals.

We are not Jesus, but we, too, are guarded and protected by angels. A recent survey found that three out of four people believe in the existence of angels, many believing that those angels guard over and protect them.

Angels have a wonderful way of bringing lightness and brightness and a sense of another, more spiritual world to our mundane lives. English painter Sir Edward Coley Burne-Jones, in a letter to his friend Oscar Wilde, said, "The more materialistic science becomes, the more angels I shall paint."

How comforting to believe that guardian angels surround us, warning us of danger, warding off evil. Angels are also God's messengers and still speak to us for God, guiding us in God's ways.

Tales of angels acting for God begin in Genesis and infuse the whole Bible. Groups of angels, hosts of angels, and a world that seems *filled* with angels are found in the teachings of Jesus and in the writings of the early Christian church.

The world can't be all bad if there are so many angels in it.

---

*Guardian Lord, send your holy angels to have charge over us, guiding us toward good and guarding us from evil.*

# *Learning from Nature*

"Consider the lilies of the field, how they grow; they neither toil nor spin, yet I tell you, even Solomon in all his glory was not clothed like one of these."

MATTHEW 6:26-29

Jesus was an outdoor person for most of his ministry. He walked along roads, hiked up mountains, and rode upon the sea. Animals, birds, trees, and flowers filled his storehouse of teaching illustrations.

Jesus reminded us that we have much to learn from God's natural creatures. Sometimes we fail to learn those lessons because of our urban- and suburbanization. Many a kid doesn't know where milk comes from, what a sow looks like, or that a chicken lays eggs. Foods are boxed and bottled and shrink-wrapped in the supermarket. Who could imagine them on the hoof? Who could dream so many creatures have to die that I might eat?

We humans share important traits and instincts with our animal friends— among them a sense of family or clan, cooperation, the guarding and nurturing of young, a will to live and survive, and—perhaps most of all (as Jesus taught us)— a day-by-day confidence that God will provide.

When we disregard some of these most basic instincts, when we cease to care about our children or the welfare of others in our clan, when we clamor so much for tomorrow that we disregard today, then we become lower than the animals who share our earth. Sir Arthur Conan Doyle once had his Sherlock Holmes say: "When one tries to rise above nature, one is apt to fall below it."

---

*Creator God, let the flowers and birds and beasts and insects you have created teach me to live more in your image.*

---

# More Good Parents

> While [Jesus] was still speaking, some people came from the leader's house to say, "Your daughter is dead. Why trouble the teacher any further?"
>
> MARK 5:35

One of the most beautiful stories in the life and work of Jesus is the healing of Jairus' daughter (Mark 5:21-24, 35-43). Jairus, a ruler of the synagogue—a wealthy and important man—came to plead with Jesus to heal his beloved twelve-year old daughter. Messengers announced she was already dead, and the mourners laughed at Jesus. Jesus took his most trusted disciples, Peter, James, and John, went into Jairus' house, and raised the girl up to life and health. He admonished the family not to tell anyone and added, knowing kids as he did, "Get her something to eat."

Jairus: a wonderful father who cherished his daughter in a time and in a culture that did not value daughters very highly, a man whose unshakable faith trusted Jesus' authority even over apparent death.

Not all of us have had such loving, attentive, and faithful fathers. Everyone should be so lucky, but few of us are. A narrator in a film called *Parenthood* said:

> You need a license to own a dog or even to catch a fish, but any old airhead can be a father.

Maybe so. Someday perhaps you will be a father or a mother. Right now you may be looking for someone to marry, someone who will be a good mother or father to your yet-unborn children. Remember Jairus—and remember Jesus. Good examples from life, and a faithful Lord to whom we can turn, can inform and support our own parenting.

*God of all families, give this world more good parents.*

# Women of the Spirit

There is no longer male nor female; for all of you are one in
Christ Jesus.

GALATIANS 3:28

If we are one in Christ, and neither male nor female, why has
the history of the Christian church been almost exclusively
male-dominated?

Probably because the church, although instituted by God, has
always been a human, power-oriented organization. Probably
because it's easier to hear God's Word than to live it. Probably
because biblical texts have come down to us through men's hands
and men's minds, fudging away too many women of the Spirit.

Both women and men theologians are working hard to
rediscover and reportray the stories of faithful and important
women of God. The church needs to hear them.

Men need to be reminded that nurturing the faith through all
these centuries was not exclusively a masculine endeavor, the
biases of the narratives notwithstanding.

Today's Christian women need to recover their biblical
heroines and study them and emulate them: in the early Old
Testament, there were Deborah and Huldah and Miriam—
Moses' and Aaron's sister, a prophetess who was Moses' equal.
Thousands of years later, some of Jesus' best friends were Mary
and Martha of Bethany and Mary Magdalene, a prominent
merchant and a seller of purple dye. Lydia, a co-worker of St.
Paul's and an independent businesswoman, also sold dye. Prisca
also was Paul's missionary co-worker. Pheobe was an important
deacon. Women: saints.

---

*Remind us, Lord, of the heroines in your Word.*

---

# A Relationship of Love

"Blessed are the meek, for they will inherit the earth."

MATTHEW 5:5

Russian novelist Leo Tolstoy, along with Dostoevski, created a block of Russian literature that ranks in importance with Greek tragedy and Elizabethan drama.

A writer, thinker, and philosopher, Tolstoy is also remembered in his country as Gandhi and Martin Luther King, Jr. are remembered in theirs—for nonviolent protest.

Tolstoy became a Christian at age thirty-five and explained why:

> What touched and affected me most of all was Christ's teaching of love, meekness, humility, self-sacrifice, and repayment of good for evil. Such was always for me the essence of Christianity.

When groups of bright young people get together, someone may ask a Christian, "How can anyone as smart as you believe in all that stuff?"

Plenty of smart people have been believing Christians, Tolstoy not the least of them. Furthermore, he was not *born* into faith as many of us are; he made that choice as an intelligent adult. The gentle teachings of Jesus drew him into the relationship.

Being a Christian does not depend on how smart you are, or how insightful, or how well-read or learned. Christianity is a relationship, a faith and love relationship with a savior. His name is Jesus. And because he died for you, you will live for him in the ways Tolstoy noted: in love, meekness, goodness, humility, and self-sacrifice.

---

*Lord Jesus, we thank you for reminding us of those who came before us, those who also believed in you and followed your teachings. Solidify my faith as I remember them, and make me also an example for others.*

# Old-Time Religion

"I am not asking you to take them out of the world, but I ask you to protect them from the evil one."

JOHN 17:15

When we are young, it is easy to be dissatisfied with "the old-time religion." New beliefs for every new age are about as trendy—and as fleeting—as fashions in hair styles and clothing. Where are the beehive hairdos, the boots and miniskirts of yesteryear? One fashion critic warned fashion models: "The more of the moment you are, the more instantly of the past you become."

Fashions and trends in religious and moral thought also go out of date quickly. Look at the popular, trendy TV evangelists who are not only out of fashion but in disgrace and even in jail. Only evangelists like Billy Graham, who have kept their eyes constantly on Jesus the Savior, have survived.

Some of you reading these words have grown up in the arms of a standard, old-line religious tradition. Its doctrines have stood the test of time, its moral teachings have proven to be strong, its practices useful. Don't distrust your parents' beliefs just because they believe them. Don't throw over what has worked for so many for so long in favor of some quick-fix, sidewalk religion. God's ways may seem old-fashioned and slow and not fully into the new age—but they are God's ways, and therefore always as new as tomorrow. God's love? It never ends, says St. Paul. Forgiveness? Caring? Friendship? Acceptance? These ways of God never get old.

---

*Protector Spirit, keep me from getting caught up in religious trends that you have not inspired or blessed. Make me more tolerant of the old-time religion of my childhood.*

---

# Your Own Strengths

Martha was distracted by her many tasks; so she came to him and asked, "Lord, do you not care that my sister has left me to do all the work by myself? Tell her then to help me."

LUKE 10:40

This may have been Jesus' first visit to the home of Mary and Martha and Lazarus. It certainly was not his last. In the town of Bethany, just across the valley from Jerusalem, the home of Mary, Martha, and Lazarus was an oasis of quiet and comfort and escape for Jesus throughout his public ministry.

You and your siblings may be just as different as Mary and Martha were. At a university, Martha would have studied home economics or business administration, and Mary would have chosen philosophy or theology. One was a doer, the other a thinker.

You can understand Mary's being ticked off. Jesus, and maybe his whole retinue of disciples, were suddenly in the house, and someone had to care for them and serve them. Martha got busy. Mary sat at Jesus' feet and listened to his teaching.

"Make her help," Martha complained.

"Don't be so uptight," Jesus responded, and seemed to praise Mary for taking time to listen, contemplate, and think.

As you move out on your own, traits that may not have been valued at home, or that got you in trouble with your siblings, may be the very strengths that will be valued by your employer, or help you get along in your barracks or apartment complex, or nudge you into your major—and later, your career—in college. Sometimes our gifts and talents just need the right time and place to blossom and be useful.

*Lord, show me my strengths and teach me to use them.*

# Deliver Us from Evil

"Do you think that because these Galileans suffered in this way, they were worse sinners than all the other Galileans?"

LUKE 13:2

The crowd was trying to learn how Jesus felt about calamity, about sudden catastrophe. Apparently Pilate's troops had swooped down on a group of Galileans at worship and killed them. Did they die because they were especially bad sinners?

Jesus went them one better, reminding the crowd of a tower in Siloam that collapsed and killed eighteen people.

You and I could make disaster lists, too: airplane crashes, hurricanes, earthquakes, fires, auto accidents, explosions. Why do such things happen? Is God punishing sinners?

"No," Jesus says. Then he cautions the crowd—and us—to stop worrying about how sinful others may or may not be, and get our own lives in order.

A world that operates on Newton's laws of motion and on gravity, a world full of disturbed and deranged people, a world in which terrorism and war have become political tools, is a world in which people get hurt—often innocent people.

God is not in the business of doling out catastrophies as punishment for sin. We can bring suffering upon ourselves and our families and even strangers because of our own sin; but God is not cutting us down because of our sinfulness.

Accidents happen. Calamities overtake us. Evil sweeps over us. Innocent people, people we love, are killed, maimed, hurt, raped, and terrorized every day. God weeps with us at the profound unfairness of the world. And he urges us to repent and clean up our own lives so we aren't part of the problem.

---

*Deliver us, O Lord, from evil. When it does come upon us or our loved ones or our friends, deliver us also from blaming you.*

---

# The Judas Within

> The devil had already put it into the heart of Judas son of Simon Iscariot to betray [Jesus].
>
> JOHN 13:2

How, we ask ourselves, could Judas walk and talk with Jesus so many months, and then betray him? How could he resist Jesus' kindness and gentleness and love?

A lot of people did resist Jesus, of course. Not everyone who stood in those crowds and listened to Jesus preach and teach believed what they heard. Not everyone who watched him heal and work other miracles gave their lives to him. Eleven out of the twelve disciples did, and that's a pretty good percentage. But Judas, his betrayer, stands as a warning to us all.

John Ferguson, a clergyman and a Viet Nam veteran, saw a lot of evil and atrocity in that war. Reflecting on it later, he said, "Everyone is two people—the Boy Scout and the killer."

Judas let the killer push aside the Boy Scout in him. He gave in to his darker self, betrayed Jesus, became infamous, and made his name a curse forever.

If what Ferguson says is true, then there is a Judas in each of us—lurking there, waiting for the right moment, the right conditions to betray Jesus. Might it not be easier for the Judas to spring loose inside us when we are away from home, when no one knows us, when no one is watching us or seems to care what we do?

---

*Lord Jesus, remind me through Judas' example that my dark side also lurks. Fill me with your goodness, and keep me in your control, especially away from home.*

---

# *Good News*

"For God so loved the world that he gave his only Son, so that whoever believes in him may not perish but may have eternal life."

JOHN 3:16

It's called "the little Gospel," and for Christians, it is probably the most quoted verse in the Bible. The word *gospel* means good news, and certainly John 3:16 is the good news in a nutshell. Jesus, God's only son, came to this world to offer eternal life to those who believe.

The key word is *believe.*

Imagine ten days of a yukky flu. You are locked in your room, not quite ready to rejoin the world. Someone knocks at the door, claiming to have a bowl of hot chicken soup. The voice is like your mother's.

"That sounds so good," you think, "but is that really my mother? What if it's a burglar or a murderer or some other stranger trying to fool me?"

Jesus once said, "Behold, I stand at the door and knock." If you don't open the door, then none of Jesus' promises will apply to you. Opening the door involves some risk. Jesus will become your best friend—maybe shutting out other kinds of friends. Your life will change. You may have to give up some of your pet sins and cloudy areas. But with the open door comes also the promises. The friend outside says, "Lo, I will be with you always"; and he comes with the little gospel promise, "You shall not perish but have eternal life."

---

*Lord Jesus, my friend, empower me to open the door and keep it open. Keep me believing the good news—and sharing it with others.*

---

# Start Where You Are

"All authority in heaven and on earth has been given to me. Go therefore and make disciples of all nations, baptizing them in the name of the father and of the Son and of the Holy Spirit, and teaching them to obey everything that I have commanded you. And remember, I am with you always, to the end of the age."

MATTHEW 28:18-20

This is called Jesus' great mission command. "Go out and make disciples," he says. Are we all missionaries or what? Are we supposed to take him literally and go out and baptize and teach? Where do we start? How much can be expected of someone like me? I wouldn't know what to say. I'm too shy.

With the command comes the power: "I am with you always." In The Acts of the Apostles, sometimes called the Second Gospel of Luke, the pattern of witnessing is outlined:

You shall receive power when the Holy Spirit has come upon you; and you shall be my witnesses in Jerusalem and in all Judea and Samaria and to the end of the world.          ACTS 1:8

Around your home and in the neighborhood and church in which you grew up, pehaps someone was always laying religion on you. Now that you are out on your own, this may be the first time in your life that *you* are the agent. In days gone by, parents, pastors, and Sunday school teachers always brought *you* the Good News. Now you may be the only one in your group, your apartment, your office, who has the Good News. Now is your chance. The pattern is obvious: start where you are and move out. Pray first, then counsel, discuss, and invite. God bless you, missionary!

---

*Holy Spirit, infuse me with your power that I may witness to the faith that is in me—starting with those nearby.*

---

# Such a Teacher

They were astounded at [Jesus'] teaching, for he taught them as one having authority, and not as the scribes.

MARK 1:22

Good teachers have certain things in common. They know the subject matter very well, and they speak of it with authority. But in spite of knowing so much, good teachers do not get puffed up with knowledge, or put anyone down, or make anyone feel bad. They explain or illustrate difficult ideas.

Jesus was that kind of teacher. He turned ordinary listeners into good learners, often illustrating his moral teachings with stories or parables. He spoke with so much authority that people remarked about it, contrasting him to their other religious leaders who never took a stand on anything.

His authority was part of the reason Jesus had such a large following. When people search for truth, they respect those who seem to offer it with authority: "You have heard it said . . . but I say unto you." The authoritative voice. The final word.

Because he was and is God, Jesus is still the authority, the last word. Although some people discount his teachings and take him less seriously because he lived so long ago, Christians believe that his divine voice rifles through nonsense and speaks truth. From his teachings we learn love and forgiveness and service. We learn that what we think and feel is just as important as what we do.

The world will never again know such a teacher.

---

*Lord Jesus, teach me lessons anew. Give me ears to hear, eyes to see, lips to speak, and hands and feet to act.*

---

# *What Next?*

God is our refuge and strength, a very present help in trouble.

"Troubles come in threes," says an old superstition. We know that isn't true, but there are times when calamities seem to tumble over themselves trying to happen to us. After a series of bad scenes we ask, "What next?"

One of the Kennedys once said, "I guess the only reason our family has survived is, that there are more of us than there is trouble."

Playwright Tom Stoppard, in *Rosencrantz and Gildenstern Are Dead,* writes,

> Things have gone about as far as they can go, when things have gotten about as bad as they can get.

Trouble can be with us for a long time—because of mental problems, for instance, or in an abusive or alcoholic home. But trouble doesn't last forever. Conditions change. People change. We move to a new neighborhood. Someone leaves home (as you may have). Someone dies.

Don't give up. Sometimes when conditions look the worst, they are about to change for the better. Imagine how bad the disciples must have felt on that first Good Friday when their leader—their teacher, their friend—hung dead on the cross. It must have seemed like that was the ultimate trouble, the absolute end of everything.

It was in fact the *beginning* of everything—not only for them, but for all of us.

---

*Make me to know, caring Lord, that you are always with me, especially in times of deepest trouble.*

---

# What Money Can't Buy

"You lack one thing, go, sell what you own and give the money to the poor, and you will have treasure in heaven; then come, follow me."

MARK 10:21

Everyone could see he was wealthy, this young man; even his clothes shouted it. He claimed he had kept all the religious rules since he was a boy, following God's commandments to the letter. But when Jesus preached and taught about the kingdom of God, the young man heard echoes of eternity. "Good teacher," he asked, "what must I do to inherit eternal life?"

"You have to give it all to the poor," Jesus answered, "all that you have earned, all that you have inherited—and then follow me."

Everyone saw the young man's face fall. Everyone saw Jesus put his finger on the one thing the young man couldn't give up. He had everything anyone could want, including spiritual curiosity and a desire to relate to Jesus. But he chose to define himself by his possessions, his things, the position and power of his wealth. He wandered away, sad and sorrowful. The choice was too hard.

Position and power in Jesus' eyes come from faith, hope, love, service, and having God's Son as a friend. These things money can't buy. The rich young man never figured that out.

If you want to define yourself by wealth or things, by a lucrative profession or an important job, stop and consider. The rich young ruler lost out on Jesus' friendship and eternal promises because he couldn't redefine himself.

---

*Lord Jesus, don't let me define myself by money and things. Teach me to set worthy goals and to move toward them with faith. Teach me also to be content and thankful for what I do receive.*

---

# Ready for a Change

> "At an acceptable time I have listened to you, and on a day of salvation I have helped you."
>
> 2 CORINTHIANS 6:2

Sometimes the most important things are the easiest to put off. Sometimes we put them off exactly because they *are* important, and because we know that important decisions can drastically alter our lives.

Like kicking a habit. Smoking, perhaps, or binge drinking or messing with drugs or easy sex. There is always a voice inside that says, "Shape up," and then says, "Behold, *now* is the acceptable time." We hear that voice, and we know it's true. We go to bed and say to ourselves, "Tomorrow it's cold turkey."

When tomorrow comes we slip right back into the old habits. Each midnight we resolve, and each morning we flush the resolution down the toilet. We seem to need the habit's crutch; or we fear the change; or, remembering so many failed resolutions, we have no confidence in our own willpower.

Sometimes the only way is to ask for help.

Kicking bad habits is easier with friends alongside. Through prayer, friends and family and congregation can surround us like a spiritual blanket. We can tell our Christian friends, "I need to make this change, can you help me?"

Then be ready for change. Be ready to hit the ground running and plunge into a new and better life. "Behold, now is the day of salvation."

---

*Lord Jesus, be my trusted friend. Give me courage to ask for help, then help me to change.*

---

# The Sins of Others

Fornicators, idolaters, adulterers, male prostitutes, sodomites, thieves, the greedy, drunkards, revilers, robbers—none of these will inherit the kingdom of God.

I CORINTHIANS 6:9-10

Quite a list. At some moment wouldn't we each fit into some slot in that hit list of the sinful? Who hasn't been greedy sometimes or immoral sometimes or sometimes idolized someone or something more than God, or on occasion stolen something or some idea, or taken false credit. We all sin, and we all need God's loving forgiveness.

That's why we shouldn't get all bent out of shape about someone *else's* particular brand of sin. Sexual sins, particularly, bring down the wrath of the self-righteous. Who knows, for instance, where someone's sexual orientation comes from? Who dares brand sexual attraction itself as a sin?

Promiscuity is another matter. I guess the Bible and God and almost anyone who cares about right and wrong would brand promiscuity of any kind as sin, no matter who the partners. Promiscuity is a sin not only against God's law, but against partners, our future spouse, even our unborn children. Jesus would frown on sex as a participation sport. He would forgive, but he would also say, "Go and sin no more."

Our job as Christians is to love and care about those around us, being concerned that they don't hurt themselves or others by any of their choices. Of course, we will ask the Spirit to help *us* live lives that are free from bad choices as well.

---

*F*orgiving Lord, keep me from being judgmental. Make me more aware of my own sin than the sins of others.

---

# The Hometown Kid

"Where did this man get this wisdom and these deeds of power? Is not this the carpenter's son? Is not his mother called Mary?" ... And they took offense at him.

MATTHEW 13:55-57

When Jesus tried to teach or heal in his hometown of Nazareth, he could not, because there was so little faith. Once, in the synagogue, the townspeople accused him of blasphemy; they took him to a hillside and meant to throw him over to his death.

They knew him too well at home. "A prophet," he said, "is not without honor except in his own country and in his own house" (Matthew 13:57).

The people of Nazareth never knew the real Jesus. They only knew the carpenter's kid, Mary's son, the young man who hung around the synagogue.

Maybe the people in your hometown don't know the real you either. Maybe you haven't let them. Maybe the real you wasn't obvious back then and is still evolving. Perhaps you wish your town and your old friends would notice and accept you.

It didn't matter very much that Jesus wasn't well received in his hometown. His life's work did not depend on that. Yours may not either. More important is to learn where God *does* want you to live and work, and what service he wants you to pour your life into. If, through meditation, consultation and prayer, you can discover that and then act on it, the folks back home will surely hear of it sooner or later.

*Show me, Lord, my paths of service, however far from home they may lead me.*

# *Public and Private*

"But whenever you pray, go into your room and shut the door and pray to your Father who is in secret; and your Father who sees in secret will reward you."

MATTHEW 6:6

How showy and open should I be about my religious faith? It's hard to strike a balance. On the one hand, we are commanded by Jesus and the Scriptures to make disciples of others—which means witnessing, speaking up, acting out, being obvious enough about our faith so that they will notice.

But then we get to a text like the one above, where Jesus tells us to practice our prayers in secret, just between God and me, just the two of us.

We need some of each—public and private demonstrations of faith—but we ought always to examine our reasons for choosing either. It is possible, when making a show of my faith, to do so selfishly, trying proudly to demonstrate to the world that, yes, I do have a relationship with God. Putting on such a show is seldom necessary. Better witnessing is done, not for myself, but for others, and often quietly—by listening, helping, getting involved, demonstrating the joy of my own faith by living it. Others see that and, when they are ready, will want us to share it. Then we speak to a mind prepared to listen.

The private side of faith is easier. Going off to a corner and having God to myself for a moment or two offends no one and makes no scenes. No one else need know about it or hear it. I ought not neglect that side of my devotional discipline either.

---

*Hear my prayer, O God, when it is shouted, when it is whispered, and even when it is unspoken.*

---

# *Profoundly Loved*

Beloved, let us love one another; because love is from God, and everyone who loves is born of God and knows God . . . . In this is love, not that we loved God but that he loved us and sent his Son to be the atoning sacrifice for our sins. Beloved, since God loved us so much, we also ought to love one another.

1 JOHN 4:7-11

Love is of God; but there are so many kinds of love. The "I love you" spoken in a warm moment to one's sweetheart is not the same as the "I love you" we might say or feel toward a parent or a sibling. Both are different than the feelings we have when helping a friend: "Why are you doing this?" "Because I love you."

All real love is of God. When we love, we show we are born of God. Love wants the best for the other person, and that's how to measure the spirituality and sincerity of romantic love. If the love seems only to take or receive or seek some sort of self-gratification, it is not love—at least not the kind of love John is describing in the Bible verses above.

Behind and underneath all these models of good and godly love is the model of Jesus. Because God gave his beloved Son, because Jesus loved us even unto death, we exist in a constant awareness of that love. We are so profoundly loved and so deeply aware of that love, that we are empowered to reach out in thankfulness and love toward others.

Pray to be filled with God's love. There is nothing more important to a rich and full life than to know you are loved by God and can share that love with others. Whoever loves is born of God and knows God.

---

*God of love, I thank you for giving Jesus to die for me and for us all. Teach me his love, that I might reach out in love for others.*

---

# In Spirit and Truth

Peter said to Jesus, "Lord, it is good for us to be here. If you wish, I will make three dwellings here, one for you, and one for Moses, and one for Elijah."

MATTHEW 17:4

The mountaintop transfiguration of Jesus was dazzling. He appeared as bright as light, and with him stood Moses and Elijah. The inner circle of disciples, Peter, James, and John, saw it all.

Peter wanted to mark the moment, to record and institutionalize it by building booths, grottos, on the mountain. Perhaps if he had, the monuments would be there to this day, with all the commercialism and hype of other places of religious pilgrimage.

"There it is," the guide would point. "There, on that spot, Jesus was transfigured."

Peter didn't build any booths. They didn't even discuss it, because a cloud overshadowed them and a voice overpowered them: "This is my beloved Son."

We need to go up on the mountain from time to time. There we are refueled; there we share with other Christians high experience. But we can't stay there, nor can we institutionalize the experience. The Samaritan woman at Jacob's well asked Jesus where to build a temple. "God is spirit," Jesus reminded her, "and should be worshipped in spirit and in truth" (John 4:24). Too many buildings and grottos and memorials and pilgrimages sometimes muddy that message. We are more apt to find Jesus where his work is happening: on the streets, in the shops and factories, in hospitals and ophanages—places of counsel, help, healing, sharing, listening.

---

*Teach me, transfigured Lord, to worship in spirit and in truth.*

---

# I Want You

You are a chosen race, a royal priesthood, a holy nation, God's own people, in order that you may proclaim the mighty acts of him who called you out of darkness into his marvelous light.

1 PETER 2:9

God made a covenant with Abraham, and the Jews have been a chosen people ever since. Because we believe Jesus to be the Messiah, we now share in that covenant. We Christians, too, are chosen.

Think back on times you have been chosen—or maybe not chosen. Do you remember recess in grade school and the team games? Two people were chosen "captains," and then they chose up sides. Remember what it felt like to be chosen first or second? Remember what it felt like to be chosen last, or maybe being made to feel semi-useless by being horse-traded in the last group: "Give us him and you can have those three"?

We Christians should raise up thankful hands to God every day, screaming for joy because we have been chosen—handpicked. "I want you, Jenny!" "I want you, Scott!" Jesus says, not only pointing to you, but putting his arm around your shoulder and welcoming you onto his team.

What a great feeling. What a great idea—to be chosen by Jesus for the first team, and to be chosen by name. It makes us want to play our best.

As members of Jesus' team, we do as Peter reminds us: we declare the wonderful deeds "of him who called [us] out of darkness into his marvelous light."

---

*Savior Lord, thank you for choosing me. Thank you for seeing, as no one else has seen, my value, my worth, my need to be chosen.*

---

# No More Kid Stuff?

"Unless you change and become like children, you will never enter the kingdom of heaven."

MATTHEW 18:3

Now that you are leaving or have left home, you may be telling yourself to grow up. No more immature goof-ups. No more acting like a kid. No more expecting someone to look after you, clean up after you, get you up in the morning, and kiss you goodnight. You have moved out into the adult world. This is it. No more kid stuff. Well, maybe ...

Some parts of being a child were pretty disgusting, but some parts we should be slow to give up. Jesus valued and called attention to children. When he did so, he surely wasn't inviting us to be childish: mean, selfish, peevish, moody, and all the other things kids can be at their worst.

Being childlike is different. Jesus pointed to a little child in Galilee and said, "You have to become like that or you haven't got a prayer."

What traits are in a child that we should emulate? Trust, maybe. Faith, maybe. Openness. Honesty. Willingness to be led, even carried. Knowing for sure that we can't make it on our own. Being without power and without place except when connected with our family. That's why Jesus had such a soft spot for kids—and why he told us all to take special care of them.

Moving out on your own will mean giving up childishness, but Jesus reminds us that we should never give up our child-like-ness.

---

*Lord Jesus, teach all your children to be childlike—even those of us who are older.*

---

# One of Us

For we do not have a high priest who is unable to sympathize with our weaknesses, but we have one who in every respect has been tested as we are, yet without sin. Let us therefore approach the throne of grace with boldness.

HEBREWS 4:15-16

Many of you may have spent the last few years looking at parents and teachers and other adults and thinking, "How could you possibly understand what I'm going through?" Had you said it out loud, they might have answered, "I was young once, too."

That's what the writer of Hebrews tells us about Jesus. Before Jesus lived and worked among us, a lot of the faithful must have thought that a divine and otherworldly God couldn't possibly understand what we humans go through here on earth.

But Jesus lived among us: he was one of us. He was born of a woman. He grew up as a child. He was a part of a normal family—at least as normal as a family could have been with a precocious kid like Jesus. He had friends and enemies. He had hopes and dreams and aspirations. He saw both the blessed and the sordid sides of life. He was tempted as we are, the text tells us, but without sinning.

So we have an advocate with God who is one of us. We no longer have to come before the throne of God as creatures who are entirely other, absolutely unlike God. Jesus was one of us. He took on our flesh. He was a part of humankind. He lived and died as we have lived and will die. He knows us through and through—and understands us—and forgives us.

Comforting thought, right?

---

*Creator God, thank you for sending Jesus to be one of us.*

---

# Caesar or God?

"Tell us, then, what you think. Is it lawful to pay taxes to the emperor or not?"

MATTHEW 22:17

The Pharisees thought they had him. "Should Jews pay taxes to the Romans or not?" they asked. If Jesus said "yes," he would go against the strong nationalistic and anti-Roman feelings of his fellow Jews. If he said "no," word would get back to Pilate that this popular street preacher was advocating insurrection and telling people not to pay their taxes.

It's so great to see Jesus put them down. He did it again and again. "Show me a coin," he said. Then, kind of like a youth minister would do in a children's sermon, Jesus held up the coin and asked whose picture was on it. "The emperor's," they answered. "Then give to the emperor the things that are the emperor's, and to God the things that are God's."

It's still hard to decide which things belong to God and which to government and nation. What about war? Should a believing Christian, one who is trying to live a life of peace and love, go to war? Should we pay taxes to support programs in which we do not believe?

Jesus could silence a bunch of hecklers quickly because he fully understood the complex interactions of the political forces. We, too, if we want to apply our Christian principles to complex political forces, will have to become committed to long-term study and involvement and prayer. Christ wants us involved in guiding and directing our neighborhoods and communities, our nation, our world.

---

*Teach me, wise Spirit, what is the emperor's and what is God's.*

---

# Lifetime Learners

Let no one despise your youth, but set the believers an example in speech and conduct, in love, in faith, in purity.

1 TIMOTHY 4:12

Paul visited Timothy's hometown, Lystra, about 50 A.D. On that trip Eunice and Lois, Timothy's mother and grandmother, became Christians. Timothy was probably fifteen years old. Three years later, Timothy was preaching to a growing local congregation.

Paul took him along as a missionary co-worker. Two years later, Paul put him in charge, not only of the church at Ephesus, but of the surrounding area. Today we'd call Timothy a bishop.

Fast worker, Timothy: pastor at 18, missionary at 19, and bishop at 20. Paul wrote to tell this boy-wonder how to handle older believers: "Don't let anyone ignore you or take you less seriously just because you're young," he advised Timothy.

Among those of you who read this book, there will be a few young-wonders. You will have skills and talents that will be taken seriously early on. Your challenge will be to keep growing and developing in the midst of sudden challenge and acceptance. Others of you will blossom into your responsibilities more slowly.

Regardless, commit yourself to lifetime learning and lifetime spiritual growth. You can't possibly absorb enough occupational or spiritual knowledge in your youth. Most useful to Christ and to the world are those who never stop learning.

Go for it. And don't let anyone despise your youth.

---

*Show me, Lord, a bright tomorrow, and me in it, working hard.*

---

# *Your Own Miracles*

The angel replied, "...Because you did not believe my words, which will be fulfilled in their time, you will become mute, unable to speak, until the day these things occur."

LUKE 1:19-20

The priest Zechariah was visited by an angel. He was told that his wife Elizabeth would bear a son. He asked for proof. "How shall I know this?" he asked. He got his proof, right in the mouth. He was unable to speak until the child John was born.

We can hardly blame him for challenging the angel. His wife was too old for childbearing. (Doctors didn't do in-vitro fertilizations and egg transplants back in those days.) Zechariah couldn't believe the good news.

Elizabeth did conceive, whether Zechariah believed it or not. Then Elizabeth's cousin Mary conceived. Both heaven and earth held their breath awaiting these miraculous births. John preached and died. Jesus preached and taught, died, and rose again. Both men died young. The world has never been the same.

Miracles will also come into your life. You may not recognize them or believe them to be miracles at the time. You, too, may feel the need to challenge God's promise.

Perhaps you yourself are a child of promise, born with a divine agenda. Perhaps a child of promise will be born to you. Perhaps God will speak to you in a special way. Perhaps you have been or will be chosen for a special work or mission. Perhaps you will become a helper to someone God has called. Listen for the message from the angel and prepare yourself. Believe. Accept. Follow.

---

*Lord, show me and help me believe my special miracles.*

---

# Not to Worry

Do not worry about anything, but in everything by prayer and supplication with thanksgiving let your requests be made known to God. And the peace of God, which surpasses all understanding, will guard your hearts and your minds in Christ Jesus.

PHILIPPIANS 4:6-7

Did anyone ever tell you not to worry? Have you said that to others? "Hey. Don't sweat it."

Now that you have struck out on your own, you have so many more things to worry about you can't even list them—from the everyday concerns of school or work or friendships ("Will he still like me after what I said?"), to things over which we have no control ("Will this plane crash?" "Are there muggers in this parking lot?"), to the deep spiritual worries that forever haunt us ("Do I really believe in God?" "Is my belief deep enough, strong enough?").

In his letter to the Philippians, Paul tells them—and us—to let God do the worrying. Good advice. Do you remember Jesus the teacher saying, "Which of you, by being anxious, can add a day to your span of life?"

"Prayer and supplication *with thanksgiving*." The thanksgiving part of Paul's advice focuses on what we *do* have, how we *are* cared for, how God *has* helped and continues to help us. That washes away worries: self-image worries, romantic worries, job worries, friendship worries, anxieties. "And the peace of God . . . will keep your hearts and minds in Christ Jesus."

---

*Help me to listen to your teachings, Lord Jesus. Let my daily thankfulness keep me from getting torn up by my own foolish anxieties. Give me a new measure of the peace that surpasses understanding.*

---

# Lashing Out

"My God, my God, why have you forsaken me?"

MATTHEW 27:46

Commedienne Gilda Radner canceled her forty-first birthday party. She was too depressed and too sick—sick with cancer and sick *of* cancer *and* of chemotherapy *and* of sympathy.

Her best friend Judy flew in from Toronto to cheer her up and was received with hostility: "Did you come here because you think I'm going to die?" Radner growled.

All life moves toward death. Not only do people die, but places and relationships and experiences do, too. We leave things behind. They leave us behind. What makes it even worse is when, like Gilda Radner, we lash out at those who are trying their hardest to be helpful or to soften the pain of parting.

When someone is dying, anger is easily understandable, but some lashers-out are not physically dying. They are, however, suffering other kinds of death. In the emotional ups and downs of boot camp, school, a first job; in the ons and offs of romance; in vocational indecision and uncertainty about goals; and in the hourly cycles of workroom, classroom, apartment, or dormroom; in our daily successes and failures, we and our friends can't avoid some of these small and large deaths. As Christians we learn to take it. The death of relationships and experiences of failure are painful, but they are more survivable than the cancer that killed Gilda Radner.

We can survive—be kept alive—by our constantly absorbing each other's out-lashes. Good friends know that today's lasher may be tomorrow's absorber.

---

*L*ord, teach me today to look behind my friend's lashing out— *and tomorrow, my own.*

---

# *Freedom of Choice*

For we are what he has made us, created in Christ Jesus for good works, which God prepared beforehand to be our way of life.

EPHESIANS 2:10

This is a great memory verse. It has the flavor of predestination about it, perhaps. Maybe it's scary to think that our paths are all laid out for us, that they have been from the beginning of time.

My freedom of choice—and yours—keeps this world from being all planned out beforehand. God has given us the freedom to choose. That's what the Adam and Eve story is all about. They were free to choose obedience or to rebel. They chose wrong. So do we. Consistently. That's why Jesus had to come.

But there is comfort in a memory-verse text like Ephesians 2:10. We are told that we are God's workmanship. God is our shaper. In oldest England, the minstrels were called scops. That's the same word as shape. They were shapers of tales, of stories. They were creators of sagas.

God is our scop. God shapes our story, rather like an omniscient author shapes a novel. God lays out for us options, choices. We can, of course, stiffen our backs and veer away from those options—indeed, we are free to do that—but we are also free to listen, to pray, and to follow. The picture in the beloved twenty-third psalm doesn't sound so bad: sheep led by a loving shepherd, "He leads us in the paths of righteousness for his name's sake."

---

*Jesus, Lamb of God, lead me in paths of righteousness for your name's sake.*

---